MY COOKERY BOOK

Caroline Green

a Salamander book

Published by Salamander Books Limited
LONDON • NEW YORK

A SALAMANDER BOOK

Published by Salamander Books Ltd.,
129-137 York Way,
London N7 9LG,
England.

ISBN 1 85600 013 3

Distributed by Hodder and Stoughton Services,
PO Box 6, Mill Road, Dunton Green,
Sevenoaks, Kent TN13 2XX.

CREDITS

Managing editor: Veronica Ross
Art director: Rachael Stone
Home economist: Penny Morris
Photographer: Jonathan Pollock
Assistant photographer: Peter Cassidy
Editor: Joanna Dickens
Designer: Anita Ruddell
Illustrator: Tony Randell
Character illustrator: Jo Gapper
Typeset by: Ian Palmer
Colour separation by: P & W Graphics, Pte., Singapore
Printed in Italy

CONTENTS

INTRODUCTION 6
HEALTHY EATING 8

BREAKFASTS
SPECIAL FRIED BREAD 10
RUMBLE TUMBLE EGG 12
MUNCHY MUESLI 14
SWEET PANCAKES 16
MAKING BREAD 18
BREAKFAST ROLLS 20

MAIN MEALS
FRANKFURTER FACES 22
BAKED POTATOES 24
TANGY KEBABS 26
TANDOORI CHICKEN 28
SAVOURY CRÊPES 30
TASTY BURGERS 32
EASY FISH PIE 34
SPICY RICE 36
RATATOUILLE AND
GARLIC BREAD 38
PERFECT PASTA 40
PATTERNED PIZZA 42
SUMMER SALADS 44

TEATIME
ENGLISH TRIFLE 46
EASY LEMON CHEESECAKE 48
EXOTIC FRUIT SALAD 52
TEATIME SCONES 54
FLORENTINE BISCUITS 56
SHORTBREAD 58
FAIRY CAKES 60
MARZIPAN MAGIC 62
CHOCOLATE CAKE 64

PARTY TIME
CLUB SANDWICHES 66
OPEN SANDWICHES 68
TOASTED SANDWICHES 70
JAM TARTS 72
SAUSAGE AND
APPLE PARCELS 74
CEREAL CAKES 76
SWEET AND
SAVOURY POPCORN 78
PEPPERMINT CREAMS 80
FRUITY COCKTAILS 82
MILK SHAKES 84

FEAST FOR FOUR 86
EGG AND PRAWN NESTS 88
CHICKEN AND
VEGETABLE BAKE 90
SCALLOP POTATOES 92
FRUIT PAVLOVA 94
INDEX 96

INTRODUCTION

My Cookery Book is the perfect introduction to cookery for beginners. All sorts of delicious recipes are included, each one with easy-to-follow instructions and colourful step-by-step pictures to help you. Learn how to make easy lemon cheesecake for a teatime treat, or tasty ratatouille and garlic bread for a main meal. There is also a section to show you how to make a three-course meal for friends or family.

BEFORE YOU BEGIN

- Read the instructions before you begin.
- Gather together all the ingredients you need first.
- Protect your clothes with an apron.

WHEN YOU HAVE FINISHED

- Wash up all the utensils and tidy them away.
- Wipe down the work surfaces.
- Put away all the ingredients.

CLEAN AND HEALTHY

Microscopic bacteria are all around us. Many are quite safe, but some are harmful and can cause food poisoning. To avoid getting tummy upsets, it is important to keep everything very clean. So please follow these simple rules:

- Wash your hands before you handle any food.
- Wear an apron and tie back long hair.
- Keep the work tops and sink clean.
- Clean chopping boards thoroughly. If you can, use a separate board for chopping raw meat or chicken.
- Wash fruit and vegetables, and clear away rubbish and peelings.

SAFETY FIRST

Never cook anything unless there is an adult around to help you. Look out for the SAFETY TIP. It will appear on those recipes where you will need to ask an adult for help. The kitchen can be a dangerous place, so remember the basic rules of safety:

- Ask an adult to light the oven for you and make sure it is switched off when you have finished cooking.
- Always use oven gloves to put things into or take them out of the oven, or before picking up anything hot.

- Never leave the kitchen when something is cooking on the stove.
- Turn saucepan handles towards the sides of the cooker, so that they cannot be knocked over accidentally.
- Do not touch electrical plugs and switches with wet hands.
- Be very careful when using sharp knives. Always cut on to a chopping board and hold the knife so that the blade is pointing downwards.

GROWN-UPS TAKE NOTE

Every recipe in *My Cookery Book* has been created with simplicity, yet effectiveness, in mind. However, some potentially dangerous items such as sharp knives and ovens do need to be used. Obviously, your involvement will depend on the age and ability of your child, but we do recommend that you supervise young children when they are cooking.

MEASURING INGREDIENTS

It is very important to weigh out all the ingredients as accurately as possible using kitchen scales. Use either the metric or the imperial measurements – do not mix them up as it is impossible to convert exactly from one to the other.

COOKING TERMS

Throughout the recipes we have used various cookery terms. As a beginner, you may not be familiar with all of them, so here is a list of the ones we have used with helpful comments to describe each one.

Boil Heating liquid in a saucepan until it bubbles quickly.

Cream together Beating sugar and butter together to form a pale creamy mixture when making cakes.

Fold in Mixing ingredients very lightly using a metal spoon, and cutting into the mixture rather than stirring round and round.

Garnish Decorating food with something edible to make it look attractive.

Glaze Brushing the surface of food with beaten egg or milk, before baking, to give it a shiny cooked surface and to help it brown.

Knead Working a mixture of flour and fat, or liquid, with your hands.

Rub in Rubbing softened fat into flour lightly with your fingertips.

Seasoning Adding flavouring to recipes to bring out the taste of the food. Usually small amounts of salt, pepper, herbs or spices.

Separate (eggs) Dividing the egg yolk from the egg white. To do this, tap the egg shell on the side of a dish to crack it. Tip the egg into the dish and then carefully lift the yolk out using a slotted spoon and put it into another dish.

Sift Passing either a liquid, a powder or a solid ingredient through a fine meshed sieve to get rid of solid lumps.

Simmer Cooking liquids gently just below boiling point.

Whisk Beating egg white or cream very hard to add air to the mixture and make it light and fluffy. You can do this with a hand or rotary whisk.

HEALTHY EATING

To help us grow strong and tall, keep warm and heal when we are ill, we need fuel in the form of food and drink, just as a car needs petrol in order to run. Food is made up of lots of different nutrients (healthy ingredients). The main ones are protein, carbohydrate, fat, vitamins and minerals. We need a combination of these nutrients to keep us healthy, fit and active. If we eat a well-balanced diet with a wide variety of different foods we should get all the nutrients we need.

PROTEIN
Proteins are used for growth, and repair of muscles, hair, blood and skin. Most foods contain some protein, but meat, fish, milk, beans, cereals and nuts are the most concentrated forms. It is very important to eat some of these foods every day.

CARBOHYDRATE
Carbohydrate is our main source of energy. It is found in bread, cereals and sugar. It is the most quickly digested nutrient, so if we need a sudden burst of energy, like first thing in the morning, food rich in carbohydrate is the best thing to eat.

FAT
Fat is another source of energy. It is the easiest nutrient to store and we need a certain amount of fat to protect our internal organs and bones, and to keep us warm. It is, however, the slowest nutrient to be digested. This means it is easy to eat more than we need, and too much fat can make us overweight. It is found in butter, oil and margarine, meat, cheese, eggs, peanuts and chocolate.

VITAMINS
Vitamins are very important nutrients because they release the energy we need from food. There are about 20 different vitamins, and we need a little of all of them to be fit and healthy. The most important ones are:

Vitamin A This helps us to grow and gives us healthy skin and eyesight. It is found in fish, liver, milk, cheese, carrots, tomatoes and green leaf vegetables.

Vitamin B Group There are about 12 different types of Vitamin B and they do a variety of jobs such as making healthy blood, hair, skin and nerves. They are found in meat, eggs, bread, cereals and vegetables.

Vitamin C We need this vitamin to give us healthy blood, skin and to help with healing. It is found in citrus fruit (oranges, lemons, and limes etc), soft fruit (blackcurrants, strawberries etc), potatoes, green vegetables and tomatoes.

Vitamin D This gives us strong bones and good teeth. Sunshine is one source of vitamin D, but in the winter we need to get extra supplies from food. It is found in eggs, butter and oily fish.

Vitamin E This vitamin carries oxygen round our body and protects important chemicals. It is found in nuts, green leaf vegetables, wholemeal bread and cereal.

MINERALS

We need small amounts of about 20 different minerals to work with vitamins and proteins. The most important minerals are calcium, iron, salt, potassium, magnesium, iodine, manganese and zinc. A diet containing milk, nuts, cereals, vegetables, fish and eggs will give you plenty of these minerals.

FIBRE

We also need fibre in our diet although it does not actually nourish us in any way. We cannot digest fibre or break it down, but it helps us to digest the food we eat. Most fibre comes from a material found in plants called cellulose, so fresh and whole foods contain the best supply. Try to eat wholemeal pasta and bread, brown rice and potatoes, vegetables and fruit with the skins left on.

SPECIAL FRIED BREAD

For a really different breakfast dish try making this delicious fried bread. The bread can be cut into all sorts of interesting shapes before being dipped in beaten egg and then fried until golden brown. Serves 4.

1 Break the eggs into a shallow dish, add 2 teaspoons of the Worcester sauce and beat with a fork until blended.

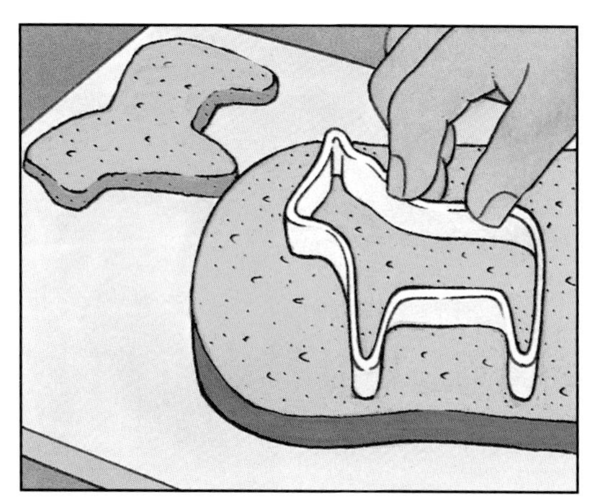

2 Slice the bread fairly thickly and cut into fun shapes with a knife or pastry cutter.

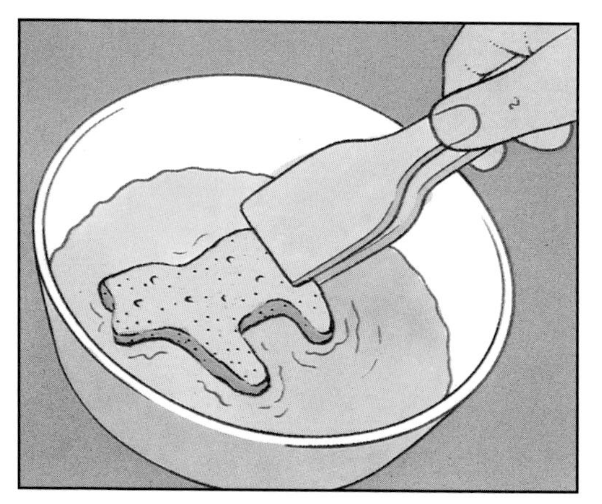

3 Dip the bread shapes into the egg mixture one at a time to coat them evenly. Lay them on a clean plate ready for cooking.

4 Pour some oil into a frying pan to about 2cm (1in) depth. Heat gently. Test the temperature of the oil with a small cube of bread – if the oil is hot enough, the bread will sizzle when it is dropped into the pan.

SAFETY TIP: *Make sure an adult helps you when using the hob.*

YOU WILL NEED

4 large eggs
Wholemeal bread
2 teaspoons Worcester sauce
Sunflower oil

5 Using a fish slice, carefully put two or three pieces of the coated bread into the hot oil. Cook on one side until golden and crispy, and then turn over and cook the other side. Drain on kitchen paper and serve with ketchup.

RUMBLE TUMBLE EGG

This quick and easy breakfast dish is made from beaten egg, stir-fried with bacon, mushrooms and onions. Other ingredients such as spring onions, chopped peppers, ham or sweetcorn can be used if you prefer. Pile portions on to warmed plates and serve with toast triangles and sliced tomato. Serves 4.

YOU WILL NEED

6 large eggs
1 medium onion
4 rashers lean bacon
8 mushrooms
25g (1oz) butter
Salt and pepper
4 tomatoes
Bread

SAFETY TIP: *Make sure an adult helps you when using a sharp knife and the hob.*

1 Peel and slice the onion and then carefully chop it into small pieces. Remove the rind from the bacon and cut into thin strips. Wipe the mushrooms clean and slice them thinly from the stalks downwards.

2 Break the eggs into a bowl and beat them with a fork until the yolks and whites are blended. Season with two pinches of salt and some pepper.

3 Melt the butter in a frying pan over a gentle heat and cook the onion until it is transparent. Add the sliced bacon and the mushrooms and fry for a few minutes until cooked, stirring all the time with a wooden spatula.

4 Turn up the heat a little and pour the egg mixture into the pan. Stir briskly with the wooden spatula to break up the egg into small pieces as it sets and to distribute the bacon mixture evenly.

MUNCHY MUESLI

A healthy and nutritious cereal, fruit and nut breakfast to suit all tastes. Serve yourself, and your friends, all your favourite ingredients topped with milk, yoghurt, clear honey or even fruit juice.

YOU WILL NEED

Walnuts and apple
Dried apricots and stoned prunes
Sultanas and dried banana slices
Sliced almonds and oats
Bran flakes and crunchy nut cereal
Lemon juice
Honey and plain yoghurt

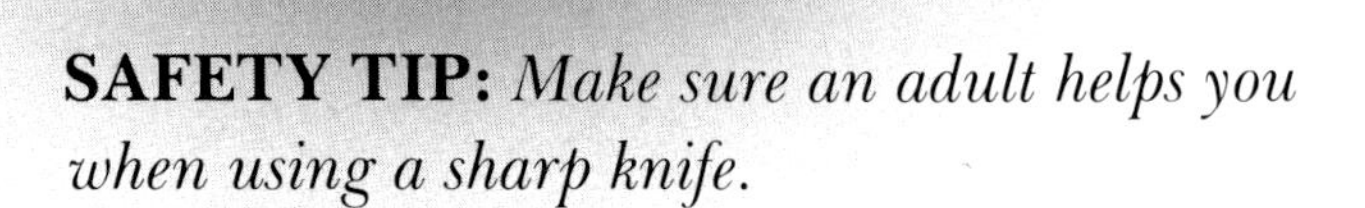

SAFETY TIP: *Make sure an adult helps you when using a sharp knife.*

1 Break the walnuts into small pieces and put into a small serving dish.

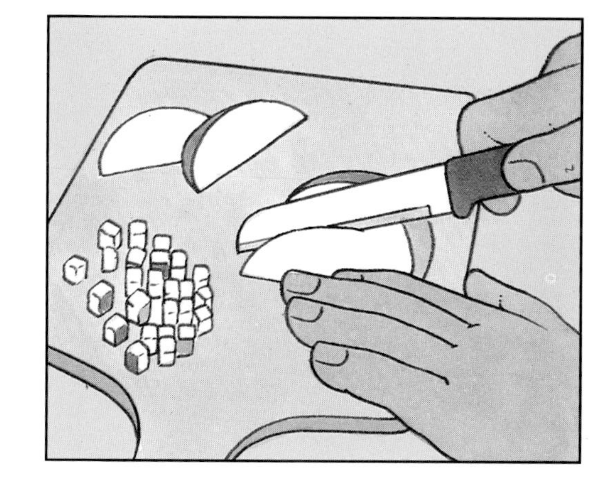

2 Wash and cut the apple into quarters and remove the stem and core. Chop into small cubes and put into a dish. Sprinkle a little lemon juice over the apple to stop it from going brown.

3 Use a knife and a chopping board to cut the dried apricots and prunes into small pieces.

4 Put all the remaining ingredients into separate serving dishes. Pour the milk into a jug. Arrange everything on the table ready to serve.

SWEET PANCAKES

Pancakes are great fun to make and taste delicious. For a special breakfast treat pile them high and pour maple syrup over them. Or roll the pancakes up and serve with lemon juice and sugar. Serves 4.

1 Sieve the flour and salt into a mixing bowl. Break the eggs into the centre of the flour. Whisk all the ingredients together.

SAFETY TIP: *Make sure an adult helps you when using the hob.*

2 Mix the milk and water together, and gradually stir into the flour mixture. Whisk all the ingredients together until the batter is smooth.

3 Heat a knob of butter in the frying pan and when it melts, put in about 2 tablespoons of the batter. Tip the pan quickly so that the batter spreads evenly and thinly over the pan. Cook for about 1 minute until golden.

4 Either toss or turn the pancake over with a palette knife and cook the other side. Tip out on to a large plate and sprinkle with a teaspoon of caster sugar and lemon juice.

YOU WILL NEED
100g (4oz) plain flour
2 eggs
Pinch of salt
200ml (7fl oz) milk
75ml (3fl oz) water
Butter for cooking
Lemon juice
Caster sugar

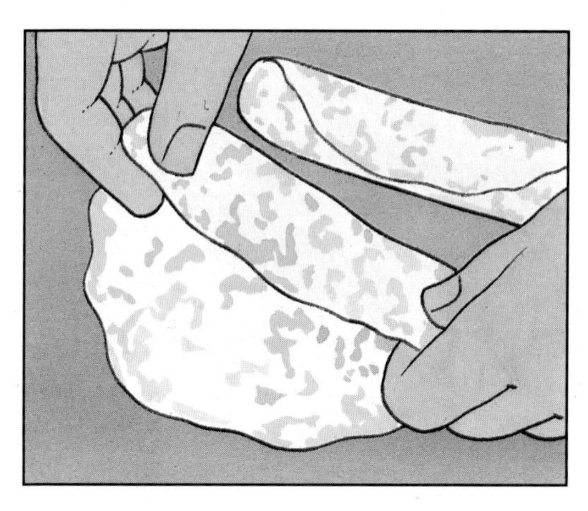

5 Starting at one side, roll up the pancake and then transfer it to the serving dish. Sprinkle with lemon juice and a little more sugar. Keep warm in a low oven or cover with a lid.

MAKING BREAD

There's nothing to beat the wonderful smell of freshly baked bread and once you've tried this easy recipe you'll be hooked! There are two rest periods in the process, when magic things happen to make the bread rise – you can use this time to clear up the mess! Makes 1 loaf.

SAFETY TIP: *Make sure an adult helps you when using the hob and the oven.*

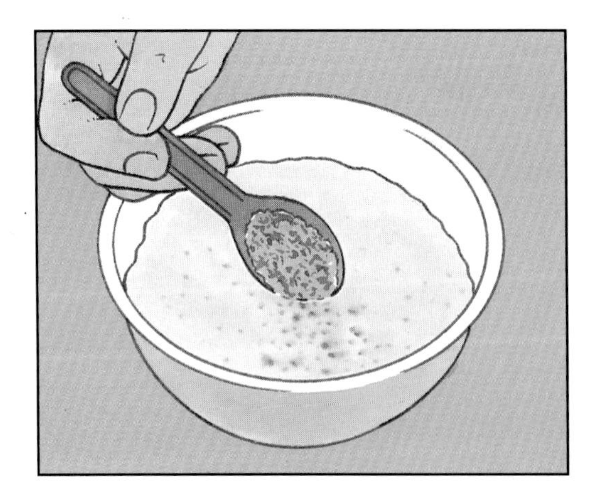

1 Warm the milk and water in a pan and pour into a small bowl with the sugar. Sprinkle on the dried yeast and stir to dissolve. Leave for 10 minutes.

2 Sift the flour and salt into a large bowl. Pour in the now frothy yeast mixture and the oil. Mix thoroughly, first with a knife then with your hands to form one soft lump.

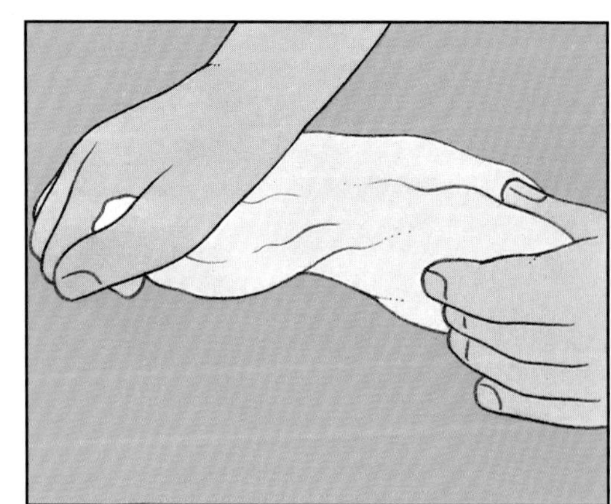

3 Place the dough on the work surface. Knead and stretch the dough with your hands until it is smooth, shiny and elastic. Place it in a lightly oiled bowl, cover with cling film, and leave in a warm place for 1 hour. It should double in size during this time.

4 Punch and knead the dough again for about 10 minutes to knock out the air. Then roll it into an oval shape and put it into a greased loaf tin. The dough doesn't need to be shaped into the tin.

5 Brush the top of the loaf with milk and leave to rest for about 40 minutes. Turn on the oven to 190°C/375°F/Gas mark 5. Bake for 20-25 minutes. When the bread is done it will sound hollow when you tap the base of the loaf and the top will be golden.

YOU WILL NEED

225g (8oz) strong white flour
290ml (½ pint) milk and water mixed
Pinch sugar
1 heaped teaspoon dried yeast
1 tablespoon sunflower oil
½ teaspoon salt
1 tablespoon milk to glaze
Butter to grease loaf tin

BREAKFAST ROLLS

Once you've mastered the basic bread recipe, why not make some dough and try making these different shaped bread rolls? Eat them with butter and marmalade for breakfast, or fill them with cold meat and salad and take them with you for lunch.

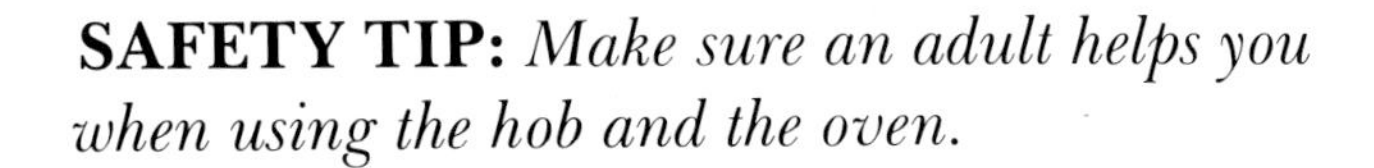

SAFETY TIP: *Make sure an adult helps you when using the hob and the oven.*

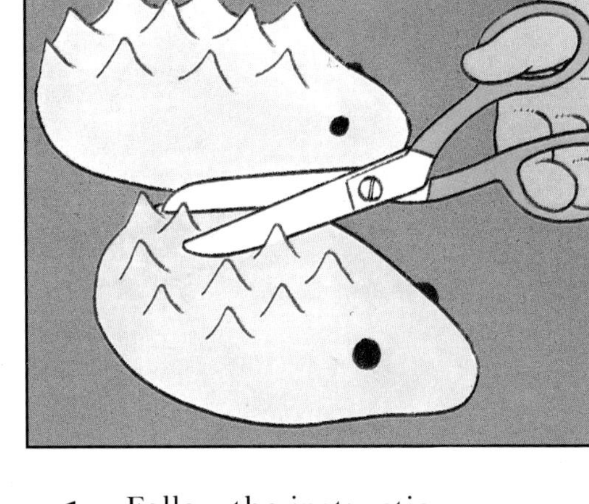

1 Follow the instructions on page 18 to make the bread dough. For hedgehog rolls, pull off a handful of dough and roll it into a ball. Pull one end into a nose shape and press on two sultanas for eyes. Snip the rest of the dough with scissor points to form the spines.

YOU WILL NEED

Bread dough
Beaten egg to glaze
Sesame seeds
A few sultanas
Butter to grease baking sheet

2 To make the shells, roll a small handful of dough into a long sausage shape. Coil this round and round like a snail shell, finishing at the top.

3 For the plaits, divide the handful of dough into three pieces and roll these into sausage shapes. Plait them loosely then pinch and turn under the ends to seal.

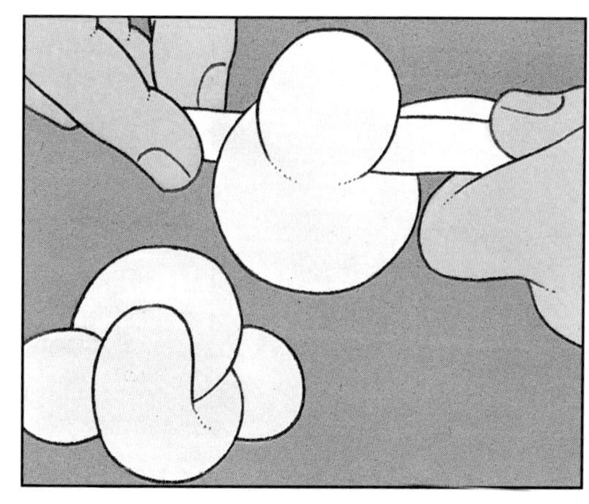

4 To make the knots, roll a handful of dough into a long sausage shape and loop it into a loose knot.

5 Brush all the rolls with beaten egg and sprinkle some with sesame seeds. Leave to rest for 40 minutes. Turn the oven on to 190°C/375°F/Gas mark 5. Place the rolls on a greased baking sheet and bake for 15-20 minutes. Remove from the oven and leave to cool on a wire rack.

FRANKFURTER FACES

YOU WILL NEED
2 frankfurters
1 tomato
Curly lettuce
1 mushroom
Finger rolls
Capers
Stuffed olives
Cooking oil

Invite some friends over for lunch and try making these fun frankfurter faces. Follow the recipe shown here or use different ingredients such as celery, cucumber, ham and peppers to make different faces or other patterns.

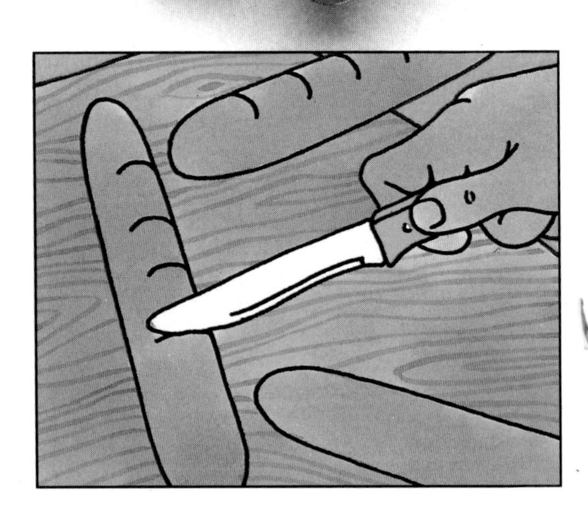

1 Using a small kitchen knife, make cuts along the length of each frankfurter. This will make the frankfurters bend as you cook them. Heat some cooking oil in a frying pan and cook the frankfurters until they are golden brown all over.

SAFETY TIP: *Make sure an adult helps you when using a sharp knife and the hob.*

2 Cut a zig-zag line around the tomato. Slice into the tomato to separate the two halves. Use these as the eyes.

3 Lay two frankfurters on a plate for the mouth. Add the lettuce leaves for the hair. Finish the face with the other vegetables as shown.

4 For a tasty snack, make two parallel cuts in a finger roll. Push a frankfurter into each cut and add tomato and lettuce.

BAKED POTATOES

Baked potatoes go well with lots of dishes like casseroles and grilled meat, but if you add various fillings, hot and cold, they become a meal on their own!

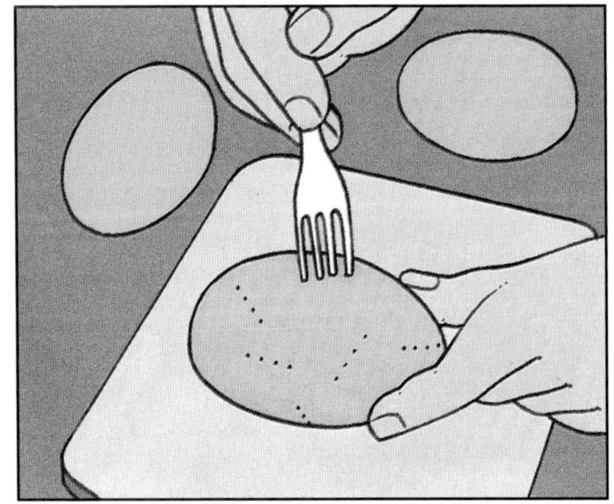

1 Wash and dry the potatoes. Prick them all over with a fork. Turn on the oven to 220°C/ 425°F/Gas mark 7. Put in the potatoes and cook for about 1 hour.

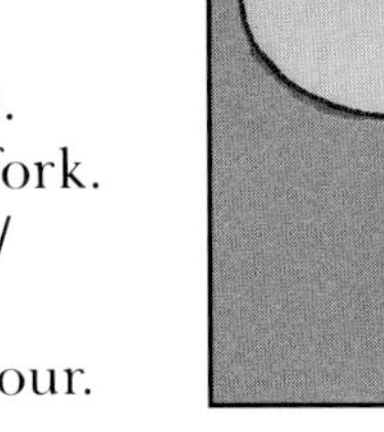

2 Wearing oven gloves, test the potatoes by squeezing them gently. When they feel slightly soft take them out of the oven and cut a cross in the top of each one. Squeeze the sides gently to open up the cuts.

YOU WILL NEED
Large old potatoes, 1 for each person
Butter

Fillings
Cooked chicken and sweetcorn
Tuna and mayonnaise
Grated cheddar cheese and baked beans
Salt and pepper

SAFETY TIP: *Make sure an adult helps you when using a sharp knife and the oven.*

3 Carefully spoon out the soft potato and put it into a shallow dish. Try not to tear the potato skin.

4 Mash the potato with a fork and add butter, salt and pepper to taste. Add grated cheese and baked beans, and spoon the mixture back into the potato. Put extra beans and grated cheese on top. Return to the oven for 10 minutes.

5 To make the chicken and sweetcorn potato, cut the cooked potato in half lengthways. Scoop out the potato and mix with cooked chicken and sweetcorn. Spoon the mixture back into the potato skins and return to the oven for 10 minutes.

6 If you prefer a cold filling, mix tuna, mayonnaise and chopped onion together. Cut a cross in the top of the potato and pile the filling on top.

TANGY KEBABS

Have a great time making your own kebabs. They're best cooked outside on the barbecue, but a grill will do nearly as well. It's hard work preparing all the different ingredients, but it's fun choosing your favourite foods to thread on to a skewer and cook.

1 Using a sharp knife, trim off any fat from the meat and cut it into small cubes about 2cm (1in) square. Put each type of meat into a separate dish. Keep whole the cocktail sausages, hot dogs, cherry tomatoes and button mushrooms. Put them all into separate dishes.

YOU WILL NEED
Rump steak
Chicken breasts
Pork fillet
Tiny hot dogs
Cocktail sausages
Tiny button mushrooms
Cherry tomatoes
Red, yellow, orange and green peppers
1 large onion
2 or 3 small courgettes
Olive oil

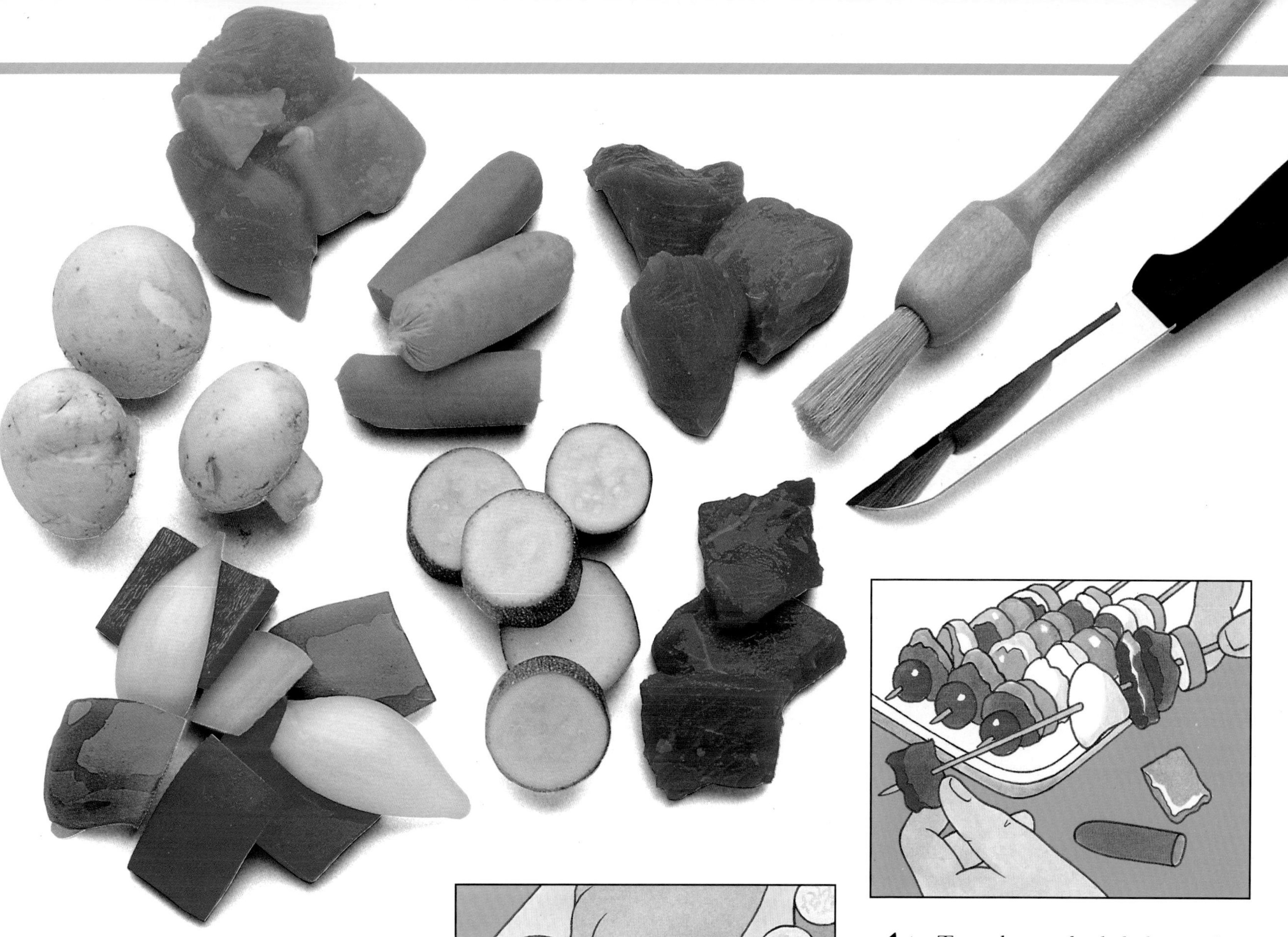

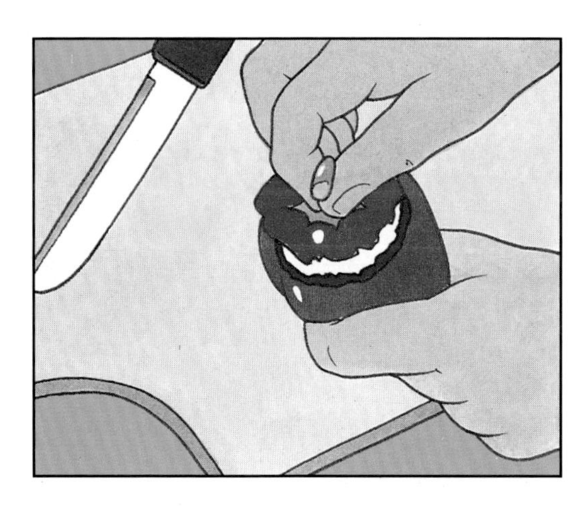

2 Cut out the stalks and seed sections from the peppers. Cut the peppers into small squares and put in a dish.

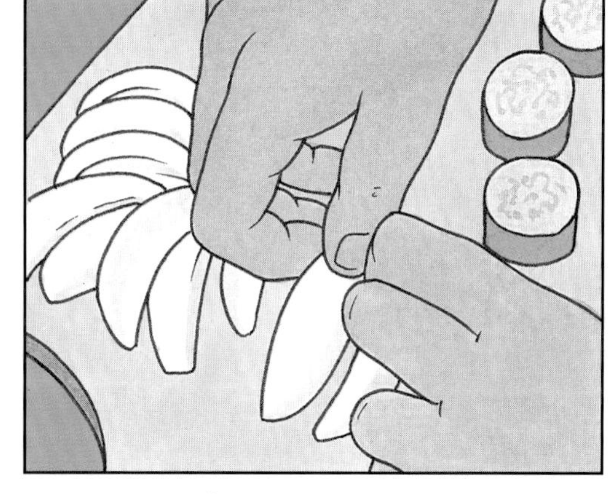

3 Peel and cut the onions into quarters. Separate the layers of onion and cut any large pieces in half. Thickly slice the courgettes. Put in dishes.

4 To make up the kebabs, push the ingredients on to a wooden skewer. Brush with a little olive oil, and cook under a hot grill for 5-6 minutes, turning often.

SAFETY TIP: *Make sure an adult helps you when using a sharp knife and the grill.*

TANDOORI CHICKEN

Make this favourite Indian dish at home. But don't forget to start by making the spicy yoghurt marinade the day before. Leave the chicken to soak in the marinade overnight so that it absorbs the flavours. Next day, bake it in the oven and serve with the yoghurt and mint dressing. Serves 4.

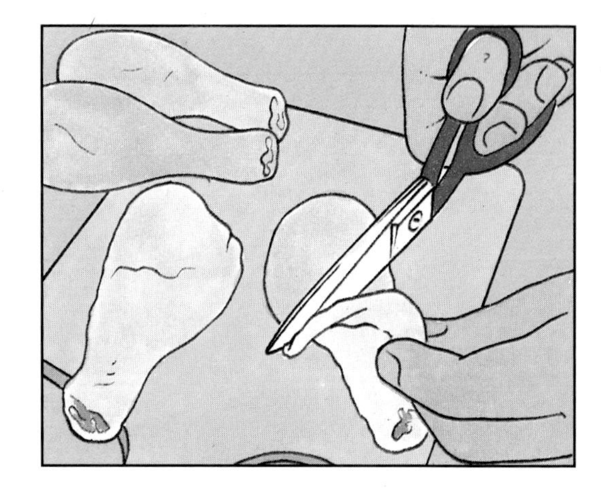

1 Make the marinade the day before you want to eat this dish. Mix the yoghurt, spices, oil, lemon juice, salt and pepper in a bowl. Remove the skin from the chicken legs, (use kitchen scissors to help you) and place them in one layer in a flat dish.

YOU WILL NEED

8 chicken drumsticks
3 teaspoons Tandoori spices
150ml (5fl oz) natural yoghurt
2 teaspoons lemon juice
1 tablespoon oil
Salt and pepper

Dressing

150ml (5fl oz) natural yoghurt
2 tablespoons chopped fresh mint
1 teaspoon lemon juice

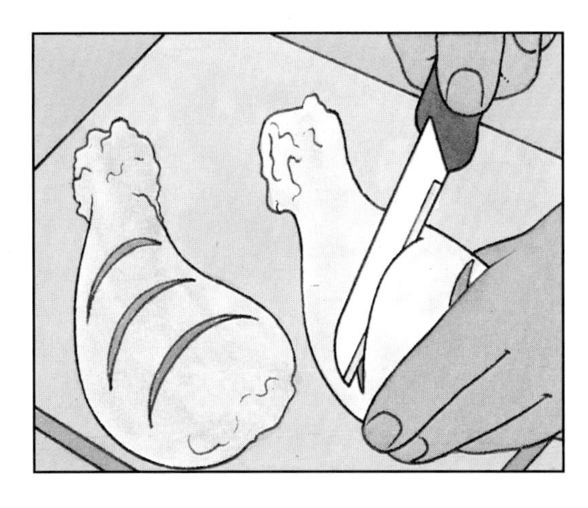

2 Using a kitchen knife, make slits in the chicken. This allows the marinade to really soak in.

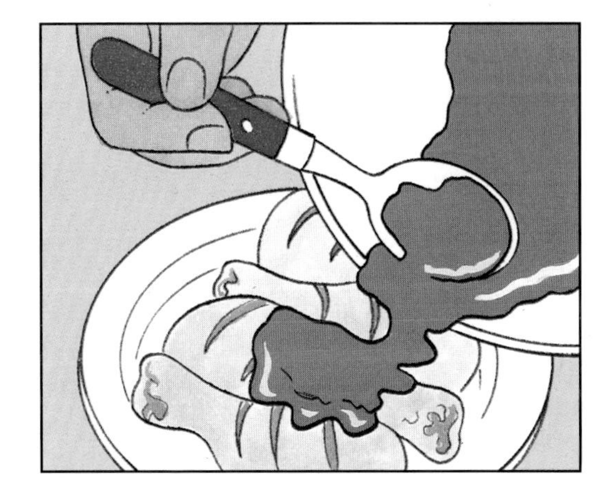

3 Pour the marinade over the chicken legs. Cover and leave in the fridge overnight.

4 Make the dressing. Chop the mint leaves very finely and add to the yoghurt. Mix in the lemon juice, salt and pepper, and leave for 1 hour to allow all the flavours to blend.

5 Turn on the oven to 240°C/ 475°F/Gas mark 8. Put the chicken legs into a roasting tin in one layer and bake in the oven for about 20 minutes.

SAFETY TIP: *Make sure an adult helps you when using a sharp knife and the oven.*

SAVOURY CRÊPES

To make the batter for these delicious savoury crêpes, follow the instructions for Sweet Pancakes on page 16. To keep the pancakes warm while you make the savoury fillings, stack them on top of each other in a covered dish and put in the oven on a low heat. Serves 4.

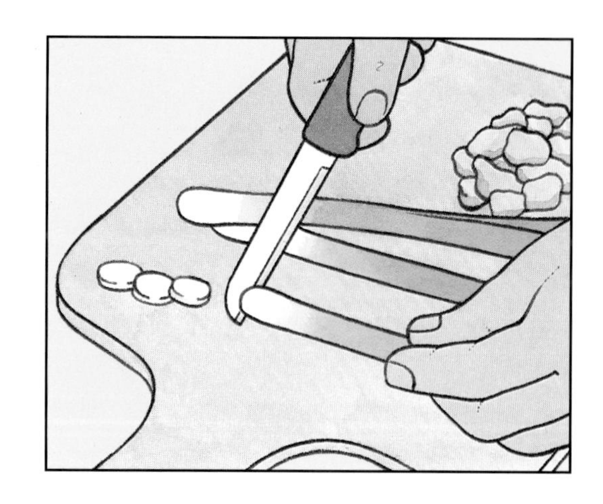

1 Cook the pancakes following the instructions on pages 16 and 17. For the meat filling, chop the spring onions into small rings and fry in butter. Chop the cooked meat finely and add this to the pan.

YOU WILL NEED

55g (2oz) plain flour
55g (2oz) wholemeal flour
2 eggs and pinch of salt
200ml (7fl oz) milk
75ml (3 fl oz) water

Meat filling

6 spring onions
100g (4 oz) cooked meat, chicken, beef or lamb
1 teaspoon dried oregano
150ml (5fl oz) stock (made with stock cube)
3/4 tablespoons tomato purée
Butter, salt and pepper

Spinach filling

350g (12oz) frozen chopped spinach
25g (1oz) butter and 2 tablespoons cream
50g (2oz) grated cheddar cheese

SAFETY TIP: *Make sure an adult helps you when using a sharp knife and the hob.*

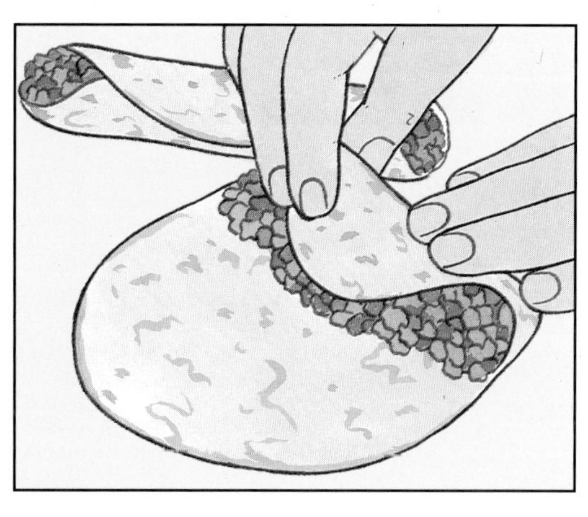

2 Add the tomato purée and the stock. Sprinkle in the oregano. Stir and simmer for 5 minutes. Take the pan off the heat and leave to cool slightly.

3 Spoon some of the filling near the edge of the pancake and roll it up. Serve two or three pancakes per person.

4 To make the spinach filling, defrost the spinach and cook gently with a pinch of salt for about 5 minutes. Don't add any water. Drain well in a sieve.

5 Melt the butter, cream and cheese in a pan and stir in the spinach. Mix well and add a little black pepper. Fill the pancakes as before.

TASTY BURGERS

This recipe shows you how to make really delicious beefburgers. You won't believe how much better they are than ready made ones. Cook them under the grill or on a barbecue, and serve in a sesame seed bun with all the trimmings. Makes 8.

1 Peel and chop the onion very finely. Mix the meat and breadcrumbs in a large bowl and add the onion. Stir well.

2 Beat the egg and mix in the tomato sauce, sugar, mustard and salt and pepper. Add this mixture to the meat and mix well.

3 Divide the mixture into 8 equal portions. Take a portion in your hand and shape it into a ball. Put it on a flat surface and press down to make a flat burger about 2cm (1in) thick.

4 Grill the burgers for about 4-6 minutes on each side. Serve with all your favourite trimmings in a sesame seed bun.

YOU WILL NEED

900g (2lb) minced steak
1 egg and 1 onion
50g (2oz) fresh breadcrumbs
2 tablespoons tomato sauce
2 teaspoons brown sugar
1 teaspoon French mustard
1 teaspoon salt
Pepper

SAFETY TIP: *Make sure an adult helps you when using a sharp knife and the grill.*

EASY FISH PIE

A delicious fish recipe to tempt anyone. It's a combination of fresh and smoked fish in a simple parsley sauce topped with browned mashed potatoes. Serves 4.

YOU WILL NEED

225g (8oz) white fish (cod, haddock or whiting)
225g (8oz) smoked haddock
275ml (½ pint) milk
3 teaspoons cornflour
2 tablespoons chopped fresh parsley
Black pepper
900g (2lb) potatoes
1 teaspoon salt
A little milk
25g (1oz) butter

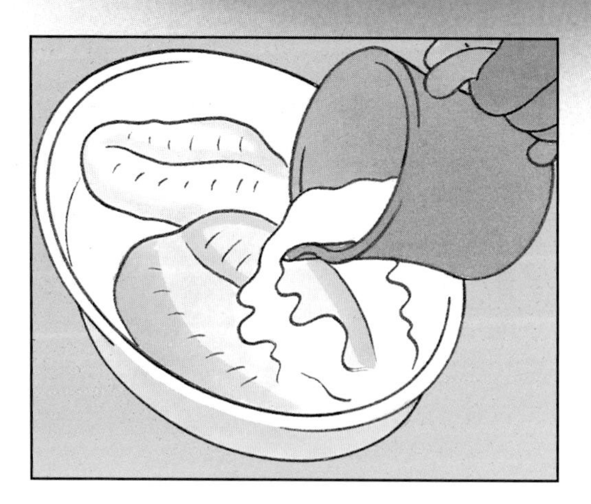

1 Turn the oven on to 180°C/350°F/Gas mark 4. Put both sorts of fish into an ovenproof dish and add the milk. Cook in the oven for about 20 minutes.

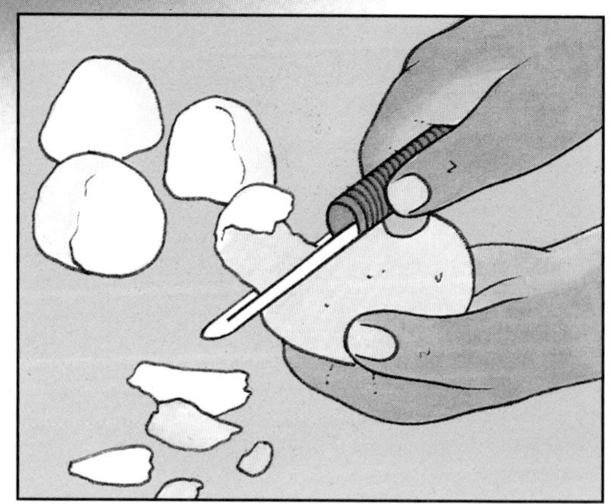

2 Now peel and cut up the potatoes. Put them in the saucepan with water and 1 teaspoon of salt. Bring to the boil. Cook for 15-20 minutes until soft. Drain in a colander.

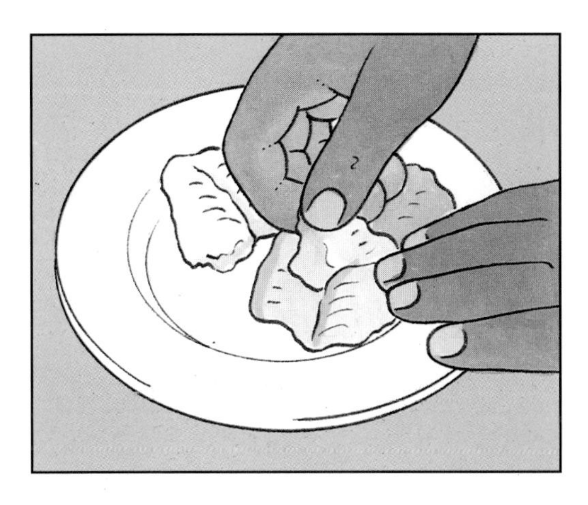

3 Strain the cooked fish through a colander over a saucepan, and save the milk for the sauce. When cooled, remove the skin and break the fish into flakes with a fork. Return to the ovenproof dish.

4 Mix the cornflour in a bowl with a little extra milk. Add this to the milk from the fish and cook gently in a saucepan, stirring all the time until it thickens.

5 Add the parsley to the sauce. Carefully pour the mixture over the fish in the ovenproof dish.

6 Mash the potatoes until smooth. Stir in a little milk and spoon the mashed potato on top of the fish. Use a fork to make peaks and dot with pieces of butter. Brown in the oven for 10 minutes at 230°C/450°F/Gas mark 8.

SAFETY TIP: *Make sure an adult helps you when using a sharp knife, the hob and the oven.*

SPICY RICE

A speedy stir-fried dish made with cooked long grain rice and a blend of diced cooked meat, vegetables and spices. You can make it delicately spicy or deliciously hot, depending on how much spice you use. Serves 4.

1 Wash the rice in a sieve and leave to soak for about 20 minutes to soften and remove the excess starch. Boil some water in a large saucepan. Crumble in a stock cube and add 1 teaspoon of salt.

YOU WILL NEED
140g (5oz) Basmati rice
1 chicken or beef stock cube
40g (1½oz) butter
1 teaspoon turmeric
½ teaspoon garam masala
½ teaspoon paprika
¼ teaspoon chilli powder (optional)
Cooked meat, ham, chicken, pork, salami or beef
Cooked peas
Small tin of sweetcorn
1 small onion
1 small red or green pepper
Diced cooked carrots or green beans
Salt

SAFETY TIP: *Make sure an adult helps you when using a sharp knife and the hob.*

2 Drain the rice and add to the boiling water. Boil for 6-8 minutes until tender but not too soft. Pour the rice through the sieve. Leave to dry over a saucepan.

3 Chop the onion and pepper finely and add to the frying pan with the butter. Cook over a gentle heat until the onion is transparent.

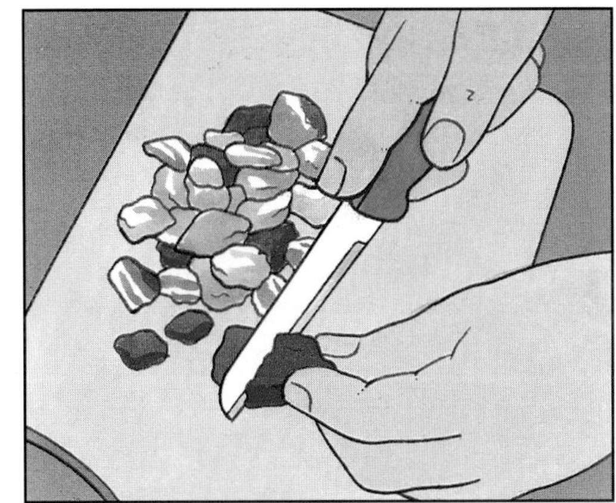

4 Add the spices and stir over the heat for about 2 minutes. Chop the meat and add to the pan with the vegetables. Cook until well heated through.

5 Add the rice and stir well to heat through and to mix with the other ingredients. Serve in a ring with a green salad, made from lettuce, cucumber and spring onion, in the centre.

RATATOUILLE AND GARLIC BREAD

Ratatouille is the French name for a tasty vegetable stew which can be eaten on its own or served with cooked meat, fish or hot garlic bread. Serves 4.

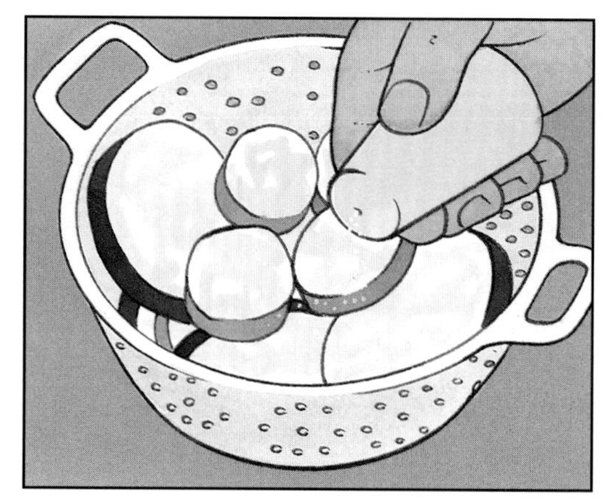

1 Wipe and slice the aubergine and courgettes and put them into a colander. Sprinkle with salt to draw out any bitterness and excess moisture. Leave for about 45 minutes, then rinse and dry on kitchen paper.

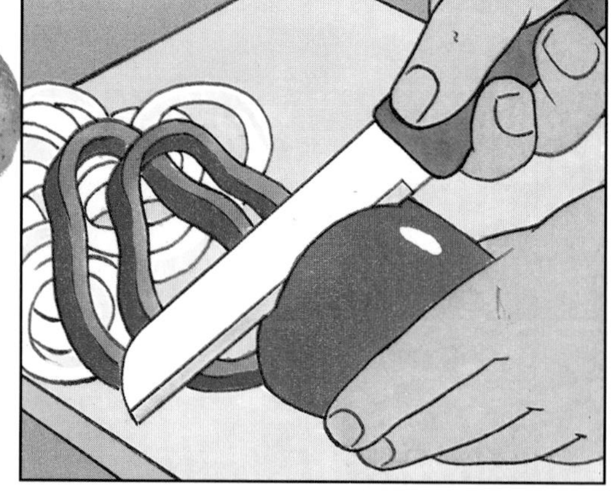

2 Peel and slice the onion and the red pepper, removing the stem and seeds. Heat the olive oil in a saucepan and fry the onions, garlic and pepper for about 10 minutes. Stir well.

YOU WILL NEED

Half a red pepper
1 aubergine
3 or 4 courgettes
1 large onion
1 teaspoon garlic purée
397g (14oz) tin of
chopped tomatoes
Tomato purée
2 tablespoons olive oil
½ teaspoon dried
or fresh basil
Salt and black pepper

Garlic Bread
A French stick
100g (4oz) butter
2 teaspoons garlic
purée

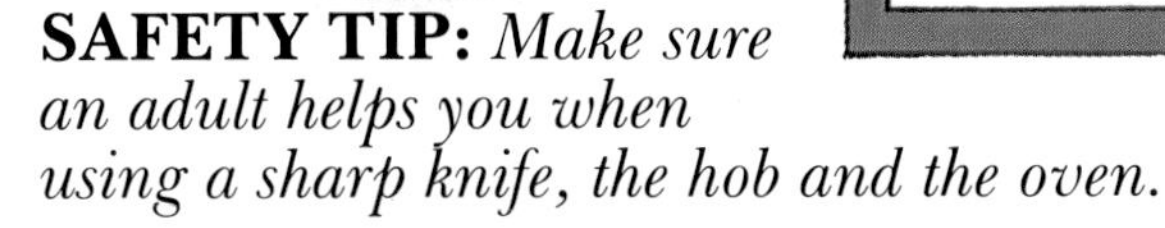

SAFETY TIP: *Make sure an adult helps you when using a sharp knife, the hob and the oven.*

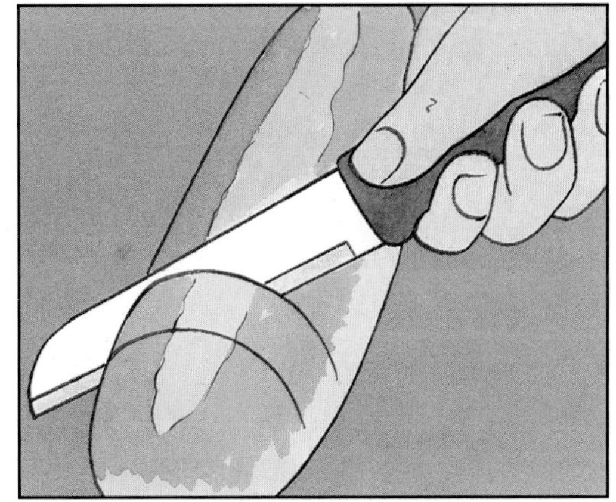

3 Add the courgettes and the aubergine and stir thoroughly so that all the vegetables are evenly coated with oil. Add the basil, tomatoes, tomato purée and salt and pepper. Simmer for 30 minutes with the lid on. Take the lid off and cook for another 15 minutes.

4 Turn on the oven to 200°C/ 400°F/ Gas mark 6. Using a sharp kitchen knife cut deep slits along the bread at 2cm (1in) intervals. Do not cut right through the base of the loaf.

5 Mash the butter and the garlic purée together and spread it between the slices of bread. Wrap the bread tightly in foil and cook it in the oven for about 30 minutes until crispy.

PERFECT PASTA

Learn to cook pasta perfectly every time. The secrets are: don't overcook it, use lots of boiling water, add a few drops of olive oil to stop it sticking together and rinse it well when cooked. To go with the pasta, make a delicious tomato and herb sauce. Serves 4.

SAFETY TIP: *Make sure an adult helps you when using a sharp knife and the hob.*

1 To make the sauce, chop the onion into small pieces and fry in the oil with the garlic and salt and pepper.

2 Add the tomatoes and cook briskly for a few minutes to reduce the juice. Chop the basil leaves and add to the tomato sauce. Turn off the heat.

3 Boil some water in a large saucepan and add the salt and oil. Put in the pasta and stir until the water starts to bubble. Cook the pasta for the time suggested on the packet but the test it a short time before. Take out a piece of pasta and taste it. It should be just tender when it's cooked.

YOU WILL NEED

100g (4oz) of pasta per person (shells, tagliatelli, spaghetti)
1 tablespoon of olive oil
1 teaspoon of salt
Grated parmesan cheese – to sprinkle on top

Tomato and herb sauce

2 tablespoons olive oil
1 onion
1 teaspoon garlic purée
One 435g (15oz) tin of chopped tomatoes
1 tablespoon of chopped fresh basil
A pinch of sugar
Salt and pepper

4 Drain the pasta in a colander and rinse with hot water. Pour on a little oil and toss round. Serve hot with the tomato sauce.

PATTERNED PIZZA

Have fun making this delicious pizza. Use your imagination and a selection of tasty ingredients to create different patterns and flavours. It's easy to make and easy to eat!

YOU WILL NEED

17cm (7in) pizza base (home-made or bought)
Mozzarella cheese, sliced
Red, green and orange peppers
Spring onions
Tomato purée
Mushrooms
Tomatoes
Stuffed olives
Cooking oil

1 Turn the oven on to 200°C/ 400°F/Gas mark 6. Spread the pizza base thickly with tomato purée and then place the slices of mozzarella cheese over the top.

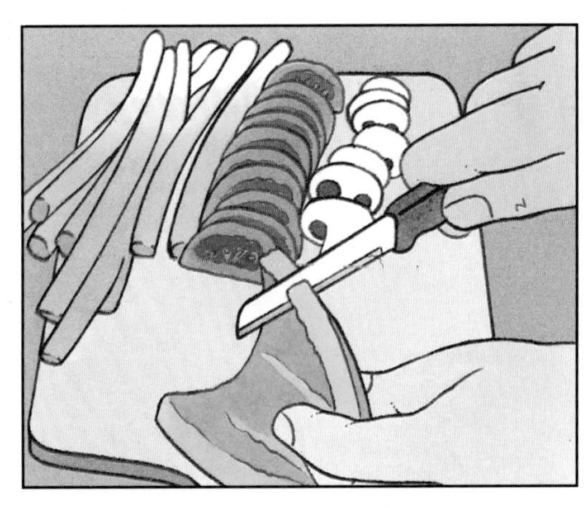

2 Prepare all the toppings ready to use on the pizza. Cut the olives into tiny circles. Slice the peppers and spring onions into long strips. Cut the tomatoes into circles and slice the mushrooms thinly from the stalk downwards.

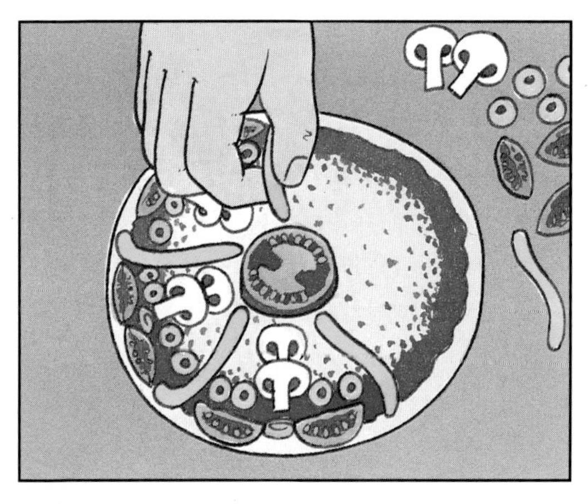

3 Arrange your favourite ingredients on to your pizza. Start with something like a tomato circle in the centre and then place 5 or 6 pieces of pepper or spring onion spread out like the spokes of a wheel. Next, decorate the edge and fill in the spaces with a pretty mix of toppings.

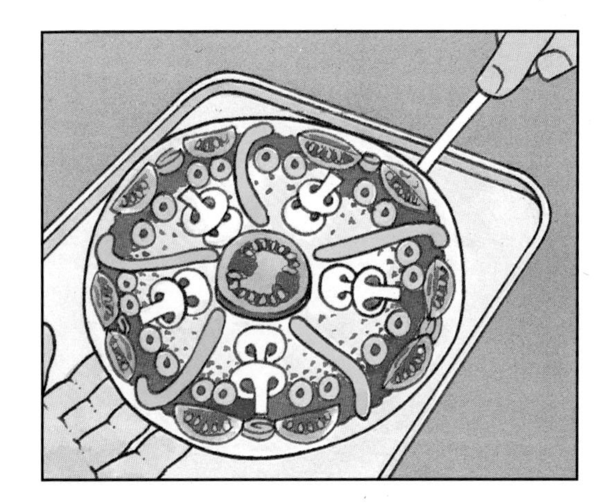

4 Spread a little oil on to the oven tray to prevent the pizza sticking. Lift the decorated pizza carefully on to the tray and bake in the oven for about 15 minutes. Serve the pizza whole or in slices.

SAFETY TIP: *Make sure an adult helps you when using a sharp knife and the oven.*

SUMMER SALADS

Salads don't have to consist of just lettuce, cucumber and tomato. For a special summer treat try making these two delicious salads instead, and surprise everyone. Serve with a refreshing Greek yoghurt and mint dressing. Serves 4.

YOU WILL NEED

Half a cucumber
100g (4oz) strawberries
Freshly ground black pepper
Mint and Greek yoghurt
2 or 3 carrots
25g (1oz) sultanas
25g (1oz) chopped nuts

3 Peel and grate the carrots. Put in a bowl and sprinkle on the sultanas and chopped nuts. Mix the ingredients together.

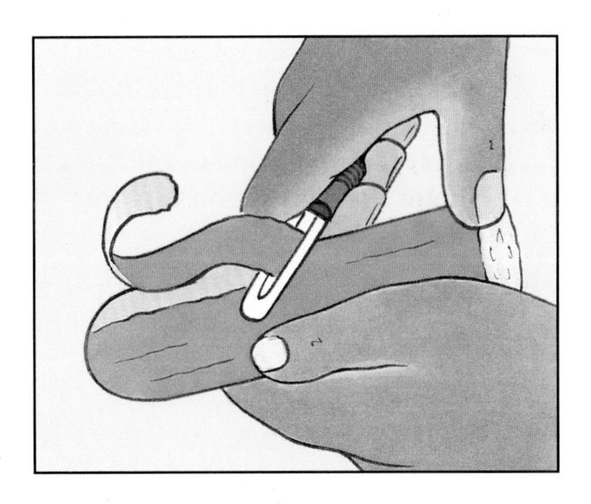

1 Peel the cucumber and slice with a kitchen knife. Remove the stalks from the strawberries and slice them vertically.

2 Arrange alternate slices of cucumber and strawberry in a dish. Sprinkle with a little black pepper and garnish with mint.

4 To make the dressing, wash and chop the mint and mix it into the yoghurt. Stir well.

SAFETY TIP: *Make sure an adult helps you when using a sharp knife.*

ENGLISH TRIFLE

A traditional trifle with sponge, fruit, jelly, custard and cream. Make it in a large family-sized bowl and have fun decorating it with cherries and nuts. Or try making individual trifles so that if someone dislikes one of the ingredients it can be left out of their pudding. Serves 4.

1 Melt the jelly in a little hot water. Pour it into a measuring jug and top up to 570ml (1 pint) with cold water. Put the jug in the fridge until the jelly is nearly set.

2 Cut up the sponge cakes and put them in the bottom of the dishes in one layer. Arrange the fruit on top and pour in the fruit juice. Spoon the set jelly on top. Put the dishes in the fridge.

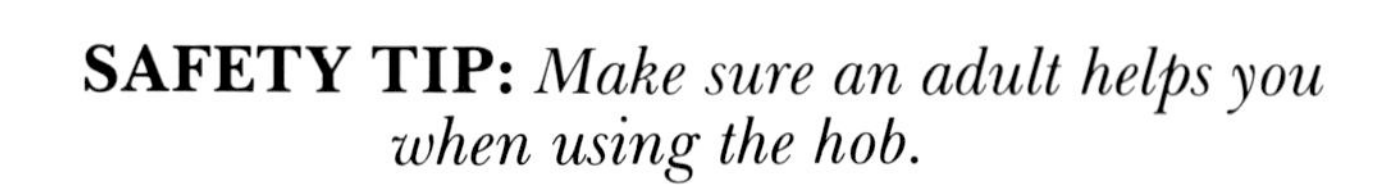

SAFETY TIP: *Make sure an adult helps you when using the hob.*

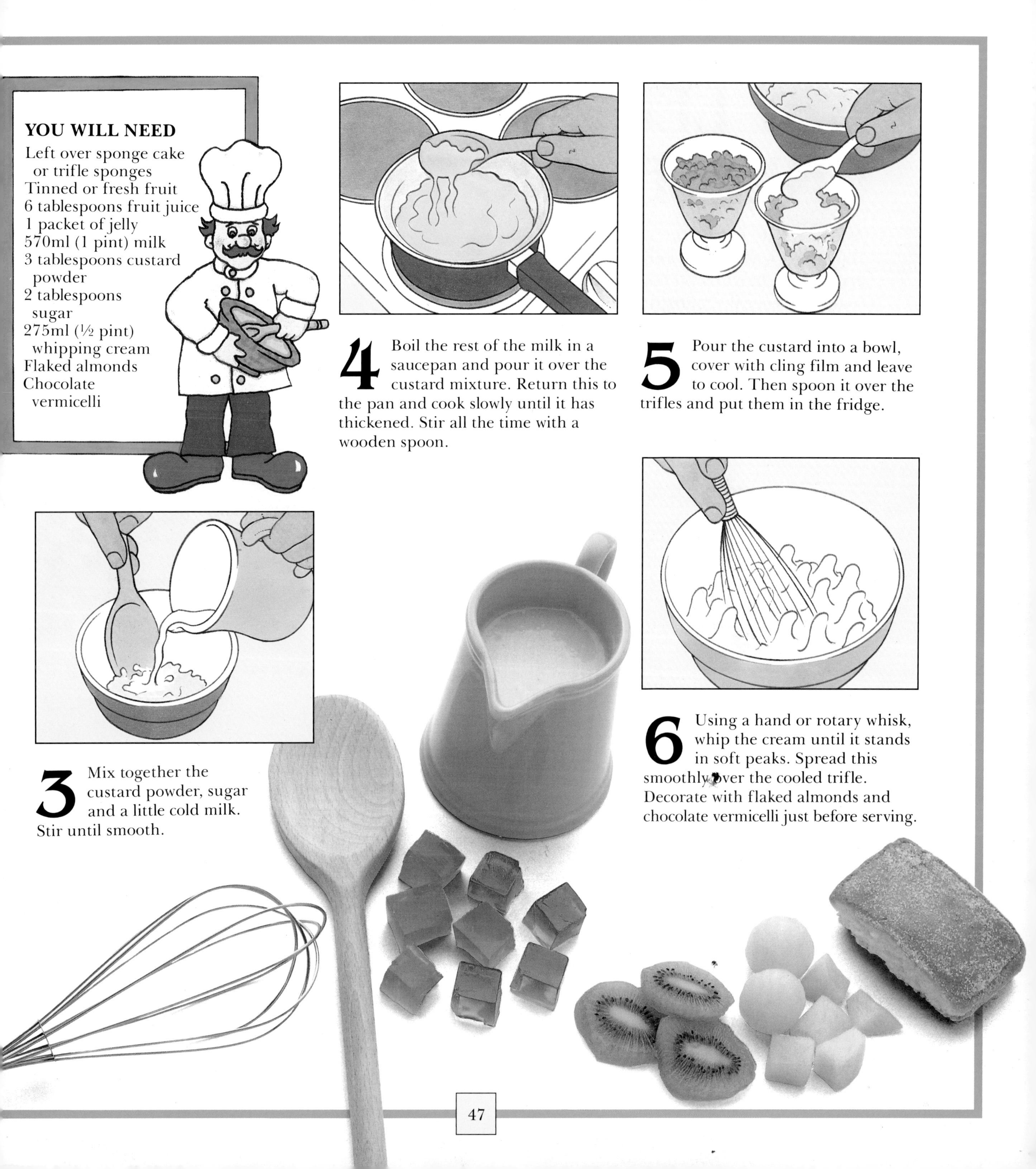

YOU WILL NEED

Left over sponge cake or trifle sponges
Tinned or fresh fruit
6 tablespoons fruit juice
1 packet of jelly
570ml (1 pint) milk
3 tablespoons custard powder
2 tablespoons sugar
275ml (½ pint) whipping cream
Flaked almonds
Chocolate vermicelli

3 Mix together the custard powder, sugar and a little cold milk. Stir until smooth.

4 Boil the rest of the milk in a saucepan and pour it over the custard mixture. Return this to the pan and cook slowly until it has thickened. Stir all the time with a wooden spoon.

5 Pour the custard into a bowl, cover with cling film and leave to cool. Then spoon it over the trifles and put them in the fridge.

6 Using a hand or rotary whisk, whip the cream until it stands in soft peaks. Spread this smoothly over the cooled trifle. Decorate with flaked almonds and chocolate vermicelli just before serving.

EASY LEMON CHEESECAKE

A deliciously light, fluffy cheesecake flavoured with lemon and sitting on a crisp chocolate biscuit base. If you like a fruity cheesecake, substitute plain digestive biscuits for the base and top with fresh or tinned fruit.

YOU WILL NEED
200g (7oz) plain chocolate digestive biscuits
75g (3oz) butter, softened

Filling
75g (3oz) caster sugar
225g (8oz) cottage cheese
175g (6oz) cream cheese
275ml (½ pint) double cream
Juice and rind of 1 lemon
1 teaspoon vanilla essence
2 egg yolks
3 egg whites
3 teaspoons gelatine

Decorations
Angelica and orange and lemon slices

SAFETY TIP: *Make sure an adult helps you when using the oven.*

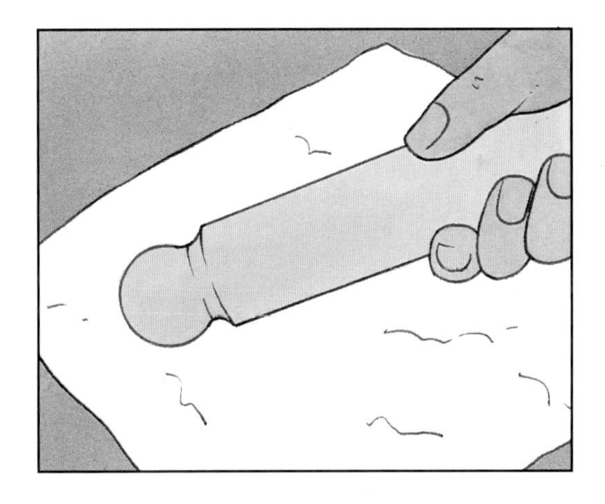

1 Put the biscuits in a plastic bag. Fold the end of the bag over and use a rolling pin to crush the biscuits.

2 Shake the biscuit crumbs into a bowl, add the softened butter and mix together. Turn the mixture into a loose-bottomed 20cm (8in) round cake tin and press into the base. Cook in the oven at 150°C/ 300°F/Gas mark 2 for 15 minutes. Take out and leave to cool.

3 Sieve the cottage cheese into a small bowl. Add the cream cheese, sugar and vanilla essence and beat well.

4 Add the lemon juice, grated lemon rind and egg yolks. Using a hand or rotary whisk, beat all the ingredients together. The recipe is continued on the next page.

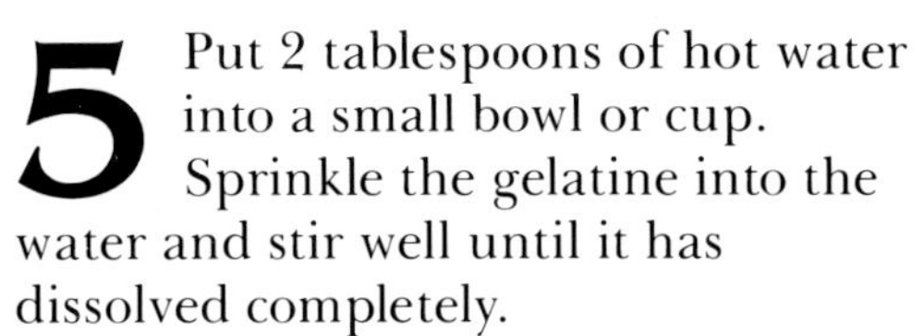

5 Put 2 tablespoons of hot water into a small bowl or cup. Sprinkle the gelatine into the water and stir well until it has dissolved completely.

6 Transfer the 3 egg whites into a large bowl and whisk until stiff. In another bowl whip the cream into soft peaks.

7 Using a large metal spoon, fold the gelatine, then the cream and finally the egg whites into the cheese mixture.

8 Spoon the mixture on to the biscuit base and spread evenly with a palette knife. Put the cheesecake in the fridge until it is set.

9 Remove the cheesecake from the cake tin by pushing up the loose base. Decorate with the orange and lemon slices and angelica.

EXOTIC FRUIT SALAD

You can use all your favourite fruits in this delicious salad, plus a few that you haven't tried before. Choose about five varieties of fruit from this selection: mangoes, kiwi fruit, star fruit, oranges, melons, peaches, nectarines, apples, cherries, paw paw, strawberries, lychees, grapes and pineapples. Serves 4.

YOU WILL NEED

About 5 types of fruit including half a melon or pineapple
100g (4oz) caster sugar
275ml (½ pint) water
Juice of 1 lemon or 1 lime

1 First make the syrup. Put the sugar and water into a saucepan and stir over a gentle heat until the sugar dissolves. Boil for 2 minutes and leave to cool in a bowl.

2 Cut the lemon or lime in half and squeeze out the juice with the lemon squeezer. Remove any pips. Add to the syrup.

4 Peel the oranges and remove the pips. Separate the orange segments. Remove the skin from the kiwi fruit and slice as shown.

3 Wash and chop up all the fruit into small pieces. You can leave the skin on the apples, cherries and grapes, but remove the pips. The rest of the fruit should be peeled and sliced into small pieces.

SAFETY TIP: *Make sure an adult helps you when using a sharp knife and the hob.*

5 Cut the melon in half and scoop out the fruit. The best way to do this is with a melon baller. Put all the pieces of fruit into a bowl and pour over the syrup.

6 Try to catch any juice that runs from the fruit and add this to the syrup with all the fruit pieces. Decorate with slices of star fruit and strawberry. Cover with cling film, and chill in the fridge for about 1 hour.

TEATIME SCONES

Make wonderful cream teas at home whenever you want. It only takes about half an hour from start to finish to make these mouth-watering scones, so they can be a last minute treat if someone arrives unexpectedly. If you want a deliciously different savoury snack leave out the sugar and put in 50g (2oz) of finely grated parmesan cheese. Serve savoury scones with butter, mild cheese and celery sticks. Makes 12.

YOU WILL NEED

225g (8oz) self-raising flour
40g (1½oz) butter at room temperature
150ml (5fl oz) milk
Pinch of salt
1½ tablespoons caster sugar
Clotted cream or butter
Jam

1 Turn the oven on to 220°C/ 425°F/Gas mark 7. Sieve the flour into a bowl and rub the butter in lightly with your fingertips. Stir in the sugar and salt.

2 Using a knife, gradually stir the milk into the flour mixture a little at a time. Sprinkle a little flour on to your hands and gently make the dough into a ball.

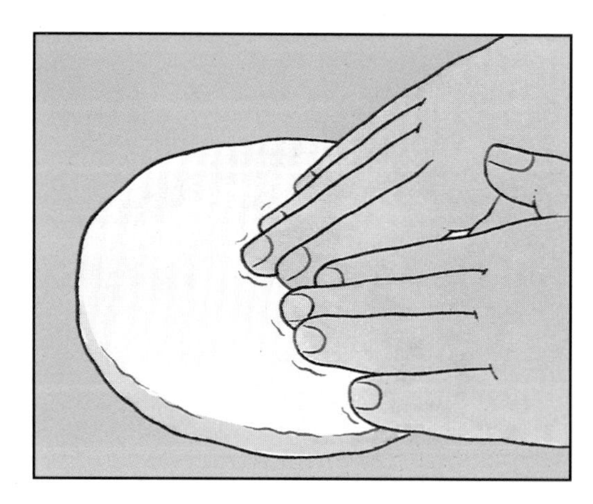

3 Sprinkle flour on to the work surface and gently press the dough out flat so that it is about 2cm (¾in) thick.

5 Place the scones on a greased baking sheet, brush each one with a little milk and bake in the oven for about 12-15 minutes. Eat while still warm, with butter or cream and jam.

4 Cut the scones out with the pastry cutter, pressing it down firmly through the dough without twisting it. Cut out as many scones as you can. Press the scraps of dough together to the same thickness and cut out more scones.

SAFETY TIP: *Make sure an adult helps you when using the oven.*

FLORENTINE BISCUITS

YOU WILL NEED

3 or 4 glacé cherries
14g (½oz) angelica
100g (4oz) chopped mixed nuts
2 tablespoons chopped mixed peel
2 teaspoons honey
50g (2oz) caster sugar
50g (2oz) butter
1 tablespoon single cream
100g (4oz) plain chocolate

These luxury fruit and nut biscuits have a delicious chocolate base. Make them large, as a teatime treat, or small, to go with coffee after dinner. Whatever you choose, make sure that the amounts of fruit and nuts always add up to the same as those in the original recipe. Makes 12.

1 Chop the cherries and angelica into small pieces, and mix them together in a bowl with the mixed peel and nuts.

2 Put the butter, sugar and honey into a saucepan and cook over a gentle heat, stirring with a wooden spoon. Let it bubble for about 1 minute.

3 Pour this mixture, with the cream, over the fruit and nuts and mix well. Line a baking tray with silicone paper and put small spoonfuls of the mixture on to it, spaced well apart.

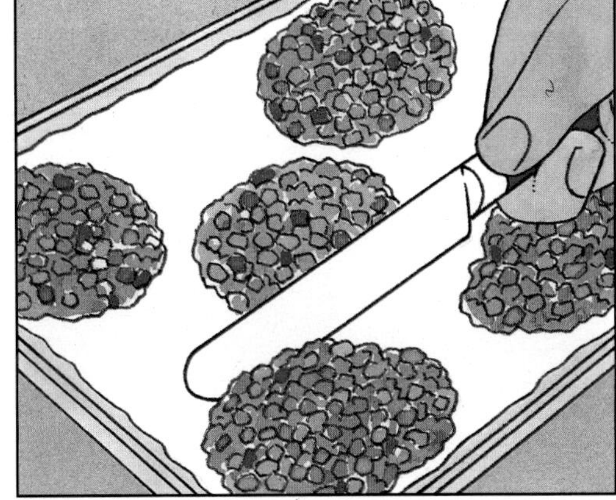

4 Cook in the oven for 10 minutes at 180°C/350°F/ Gas mark 4. Shape into neat rounds with a knife whilst hot. Leave to cool until set, then peel off the paper carefully.

5 Break the chocolate into small pieces and melt in a basin over a saucepan of boiling water. Stir the chocolate until glossy and spread over the back of the florentines. Mark patterns with a fork and leave to set.

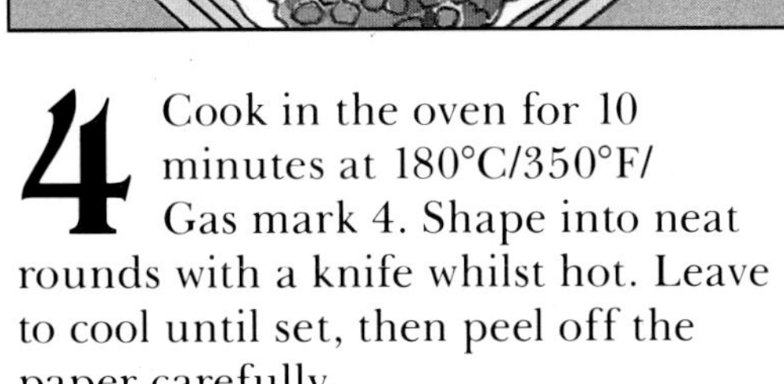

SAFETY TIP: *Make sure an adult helps you when using the hob and the oven.*

SHORTBREAD

Real butter shortbread is one of the most delicious teatime treats. Cut the dough into fun animal shapes before baking, or divide the shortbread into segments after it has been cooked. Makes 8 biscuits.

1 Sieve the flour into a bowl and mix in the sugar. Work the soft butter into the mixture with your fingertips. Turn on the oven to 325°F/170°C/Gas mark 3.

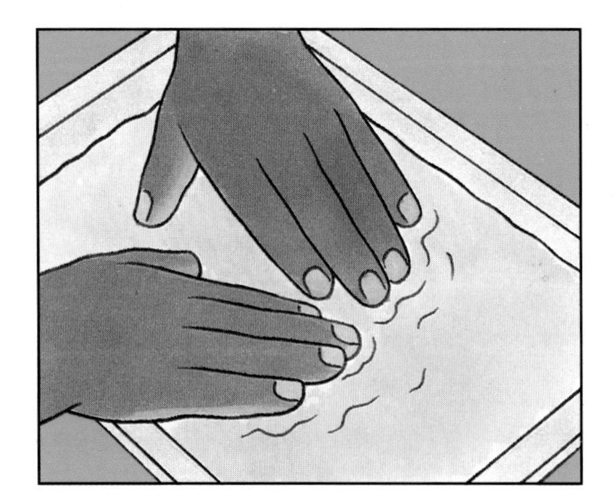

2 Knead the mixture well until the dough holds together, and then press it into a greased shortbread mould or baking tray. Prick the surface with a fork.

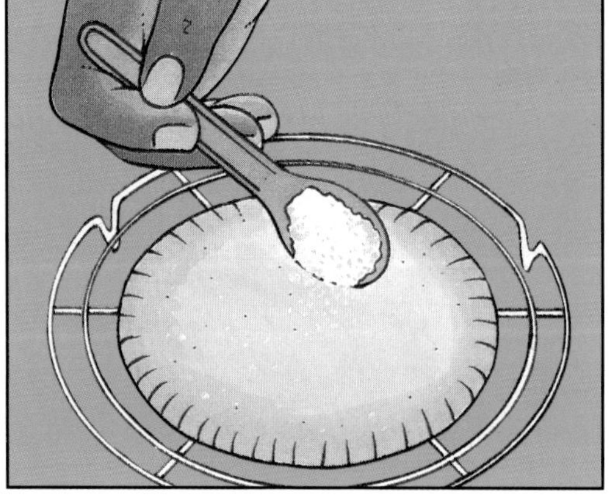

3 Bake in the oven for about 45 minutes until the shortbread is firm. Turn it out of the mould or tray on to a wire rack and leave to cool. Sprinkle with caster sugar.

4 Mark the segments with a knife while the shortbread is still warm. Separate the segments when the shortbread has cooled.

YOU WILL NEED

150g (6oz) plain flour
50g (2oz) caster sugar
100g (4oz) butter, softened

SAFETY TIP: *Make sure an adult helps you when using the oven.*

FAIRY CAKES

Use this delicious cake recipe to make one large sponge cake, or lots of small fairy cakes. The small cakes can be used to make the marzipan animals on page 62. Makes 12 cakes.

YOU WILL NEED
2 size 3 eggs
100g (4oz) butter, softened
100g (4oz) caster sugar
100g (4oz) self-raising flour
Glacé icing
100g (4oz) icing sugar
Cold water
Cake decorations

1 Turn the oven on to 190°C/375°F/Gas mark 5. In a mixing bowl, cream together the butter and the caster sugar using a wooden spoon. Beat well until the mixture is pale and fluffy.

2 Beat the eggs in a small bowl and gradually add to the mixture, a little at a time. Beat well to blend evenly.

3 Sieve the flour and add to the mixture. Fold it in lightly with a metal spoon.

4 Put the cake cases on to a baking tray and spoon in the mixture. Bake near the top of the oven for about 10-12 minutes. Do not open the oven door or the cakes will sink!

SAFETY TIP: *Make sure an adult helps you when using the oven.*

5 Make the glacé icing by mixing the icing sugar in a bowl with water. Add the water a little at a time until the icing is thick enough to coat the back of a spoon. Use a palette knife to smooth the icing on top of the cakes.

MARZIPAN MAGIC

These marzipan animals will be the star attraction at any teatime party. They are made from tiny sponge cakes covered with pink and green marzipan. Make the sponge cakes yourself following the recipe on page 60, or buy them ready-made.

1 To make the pig and the dragon, sandwich together two sponge cakes with a layer of jam in between. Spread jam over the two cakes to help the marzipan stay on.

2 Sprinkle icing sugar over your work surface. Roll out the marzipan. Cut a square to fit around the cakes, making it 3cm (1½in) taller. Wrap around the two cakes and seal.

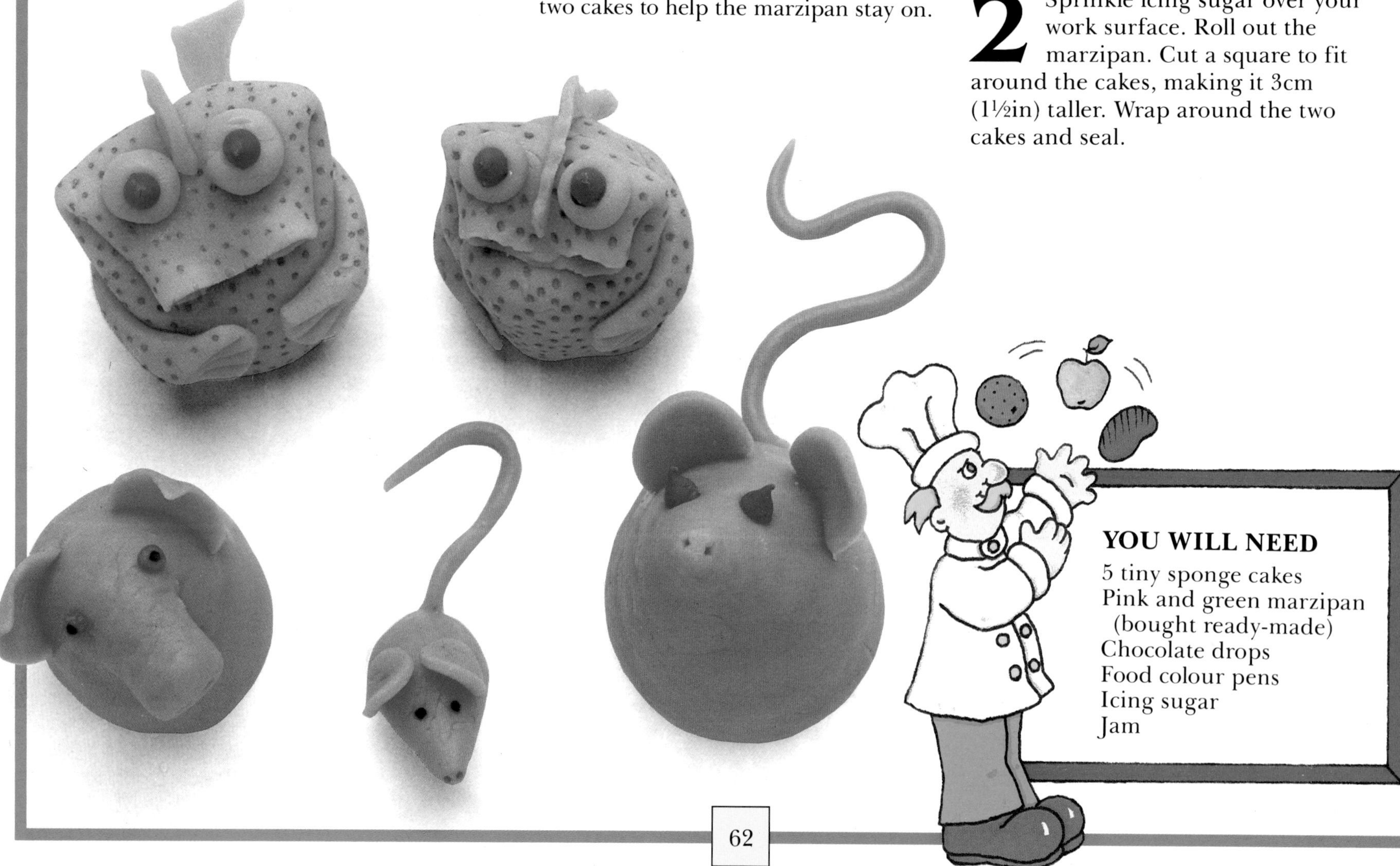

YOU WILL NEED
- 5 tiny sponge cakes
- Pink and green marzipan (bought ready-made)
- Chocolate drops
- Food colour pens
- Icing sugar
- Jam

3 For the pig, bend over the top of the marzipan and insert a small ball of marzipan into the opening to make a snout. Add marzipan ears and chocolate drops for the eyes. Make two holes in the snout to finish.

4 To make the dragon, bend over the marzipan and pinch in the middle to form the nose. Roll out two sausage shapes for the arms, flatten at one end and mark with a spoon. Roll two balls for the eyes. Cut a zig-zag back frill and press on to the dragon's back. Dot with a food pen.

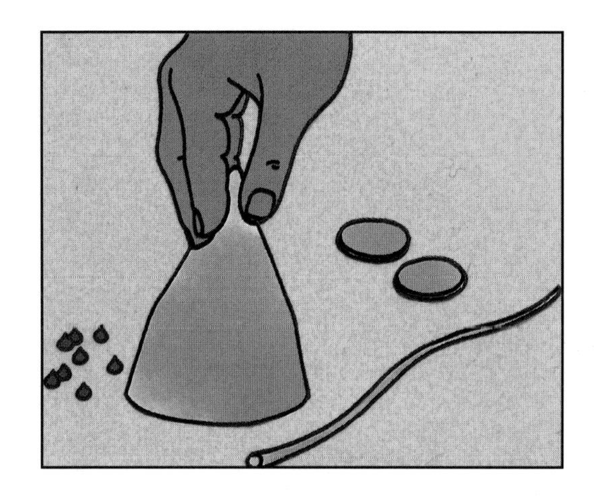

5 To make the mouse, cover one cake with marzipan as before, but shape the top of the marzipan into a point. Cut out circles for the ears, add chocolate drop eyes and a long tail.

SAFETY TIP: *Make sure an adult helps you when using the oven.*

CHOCOLATE CAKE

This is a variation on the basic sponge cake recipe. It's a really delicious chocolate sponge with a delectable mocha (that's coffee and chocolate) filling. The top has been decorated by sprinkling icing sugar through a doily. If this looks a bit too pretty for your liking, why not try a lattice of paper strips to give a striped or checked effect?

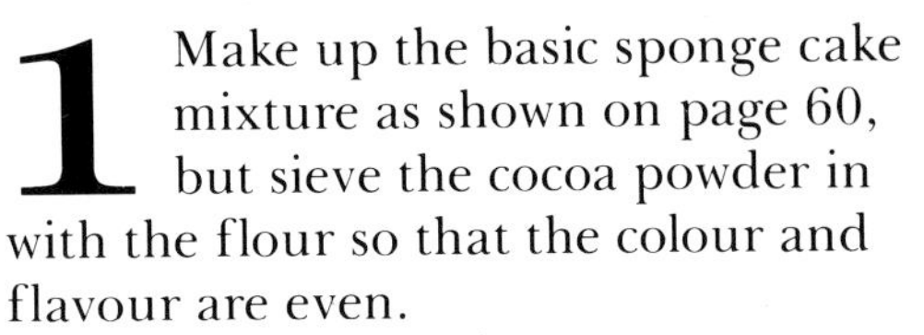

1 Make up the basic sponge cake mixture as shown on page 60, but sieve the cocoa powder in with the flour so that the colour and flavour are even.

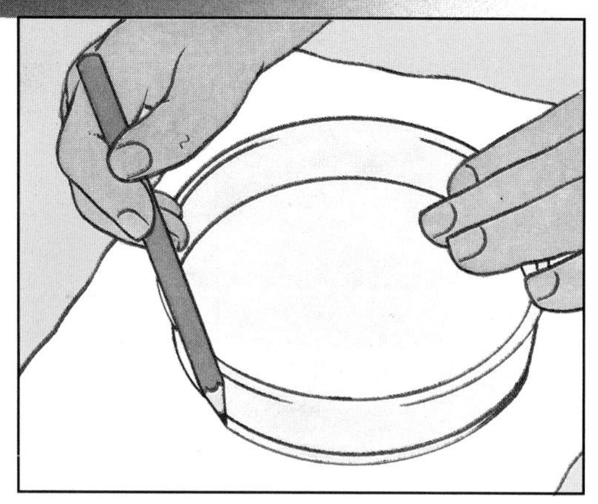

2 Place two 20cm (8in) cake tins on to the greaseproof paper and draw around them. Cut out the circles. Grease the tins with butter and line them with the circles.

3 Carefully divide the mixture equally into both tins and smooth the tops with a palette knife to ensure evenness. Bake near the top of the oven for 20 minutes at 190°C/375°F/Gas mark 5. Leave to cool on a wire tray.

4 While the cake is baking, make the mocha filling. Put the butter in a bowl and sieve in the icing sugar and cocoa powder. Add the coffee essence and blend well together. If the filling is too stiff add a little milk; it should be smooth and light in texture. Spread the filling on one cake and put the other cake on top. Choose the cake with the smoothest surface to go on top.

5 Put the icing sugar in a sieve so that it falls in a fine mist rather than sudden lumps. Place the doily on top of the cake and sprinkle over the icing sugar. Remove the doily very carefully.

SAFETY TIP: *Make sure an adult helps you when using the oven.*

YOU WILL NEED
2 size 3 eggs
100g (4oz) caster sugar
100g (4oz) butter
100g (4oz) self-raising flour
1 tablespoon cocoa powder
Icing sugar to decorate

Mocha Filling
100g (4oz) icing sugar
55g (2oz) butter
1 tablespoon cocoa powder
1 teaspoon coffee essence
1 tablespoon milk

OPEN SANDWICHES

These mouth-watering sandwiches always look so appetizing because you can see the filling. Create your own toppings or use the ones we have suggested here – there are lots of possibilities.

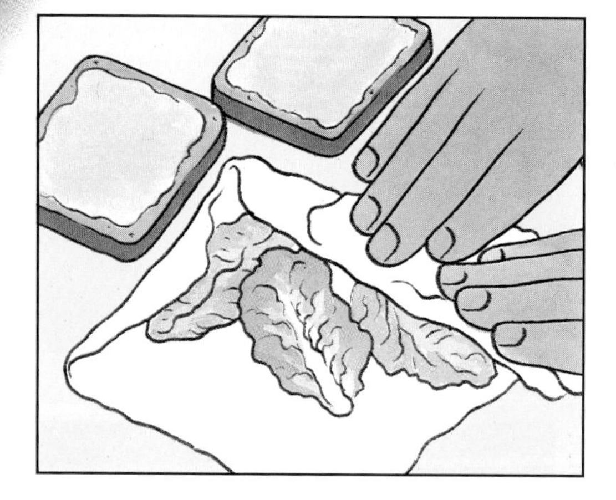

1 Slice the bread thinly and spread lightly with butter. Wash the lettuce, separate the leaves and dry them on kitchen paper.

2 To make a salami and cream cheese sandwich, arrange a lettuce leaf on a slice of bread. Spoon cream cheese on to a slice of salami and roll into a sausage shape. Arrange on the lettuce leaf and garnish with sliced gherkin.

3 For a prawn sandwich, mix the prawns and the Thousand Island dressing in a bowl. Arrange a lettuce leaf on a slice of bread and spoon on the mixture. Garnish with sliced radishes.

SAFETY TIP: *Make sure an adult helps you when using a sharp knife.*

4 To decorate the sandwiches, cut a cheese slice into triangles and thread one triangle on to a cocktail stick. Stick this into the centre of the sandwich so that it looks like the sail of a boat.

5 Cut a radish or gherkin into long slices and top the mast with a slice to look like a flag.

YOU WILL NEED

Wholemeal or rye bread
Butter
Lettuce
Salami and cream cheese
Prawns and Thousand Island dressing
Salt and pepper

Garnishes

Lemon slices
Cheese slices
Gherkins
Radishes

TOASTED SANDWICHES

Hot toasted sandwiches make a scrumptious party snack. Try making a selection with different fillings, such as cheese, ham and tomato or cooked bacon and mushrooms. Serve them with a side salad for a more substantial meal.

YOU WILL NEED

50g (2oz) grated cheddar cheese or cheese slices
2 lean bacon rashers
50g (2oz) sliced mushrooms
1 slice of ham
1 sliced tomato
2 slices white toasting bread
Butter for frying
Basil for garnish

1 To make the bacon and mushroom sandwich, cook the bacon in a frying pan over a gentle heat. When the fat has melted a little, add the mushrooms and cook for about 4 minutes. Remove and drain using a wooden spatula.

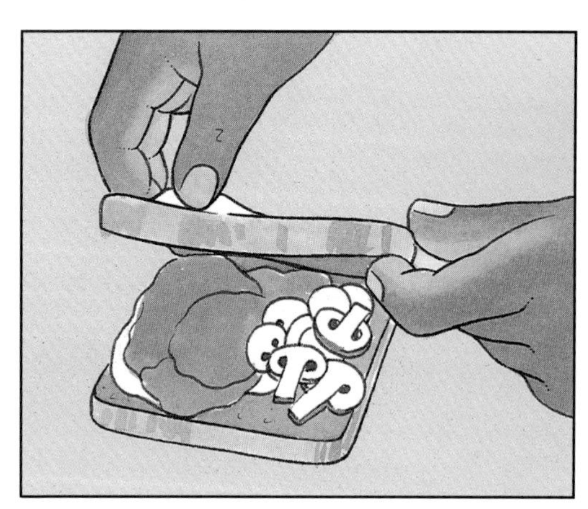

2 Heat the grill and lightly toast one side of two slices of bread. Remove them from the grill and put the bacon and mushrooms on the toasted side of one slice of bread. Put the second slice of bread, toasted side down, on top to make a sandwich. Return to the grill to brown the outside.

3 To make the cheese, ham and tomato sandwich, lightly toast one side of two slices of bread. Place the cheese on the toasted side of one slice and melt under the grill for about 1 minute.

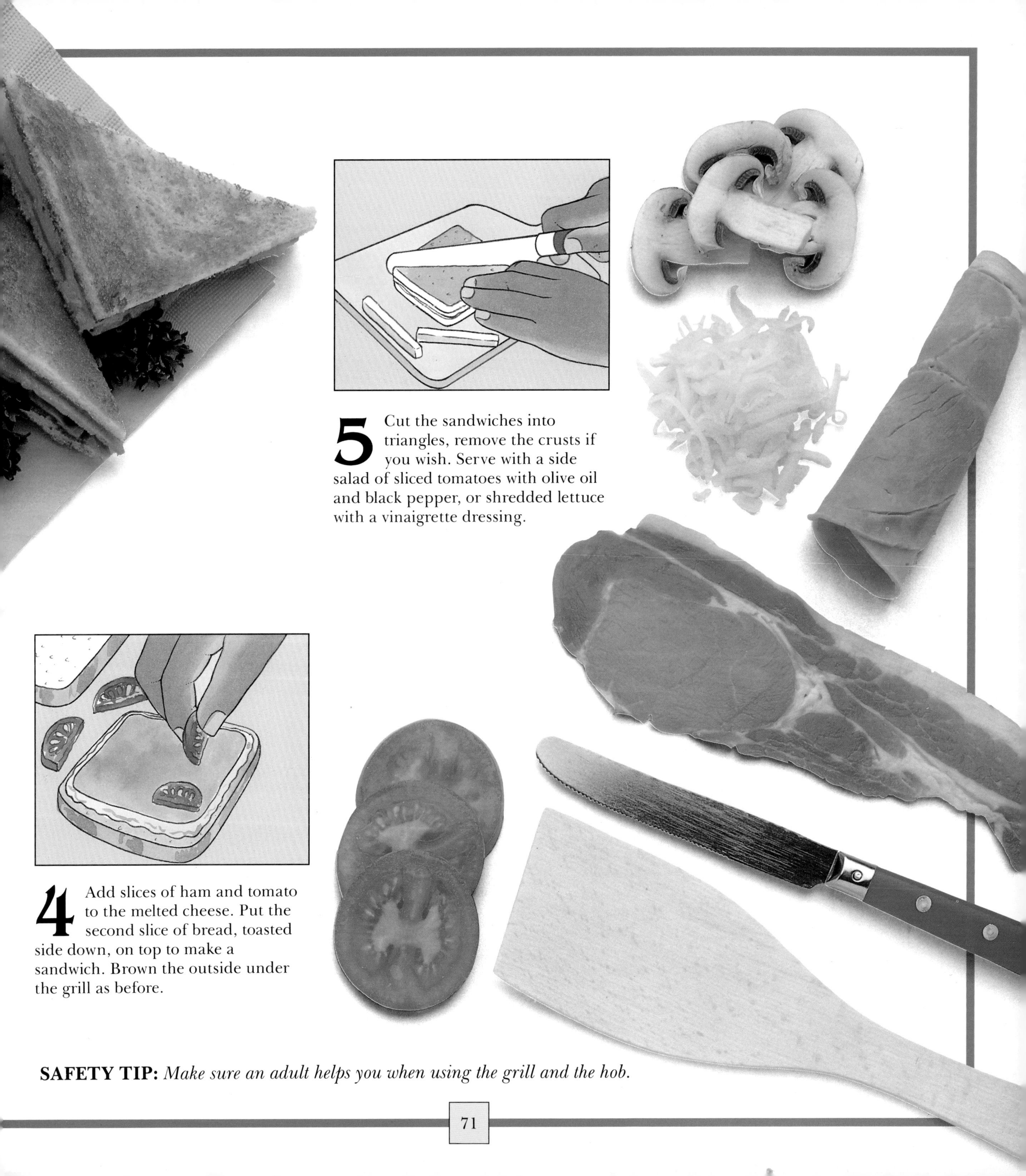

5 Cut the sandwiches into triangles, remove the crusts if you wish. Serve with a side salad of sliced tomatoes with olive oil and black pepper, or shredded lettuce with a vinaigrette dressing.

4 Add slices of ham and tomato to the melted cheese. Put the second slice of bread, toasted side down, on top to make a sandwich. Brown the outside under the grill as before.

SAFETY TIP: *Make sure an adult helps you when using the grill and the hob.*

JAM TARTS

Once you can make shortcrust pastry, used here to make these tasty jam tarts, you will be able to try making lots of delicious pastry recipes. Here are a few simple tips to remember: handle the pastry as little as possible, use the margarine and lard at room temperature, keep your hands cool and use ice-cold water for mixing. Makes 12.

YOU WILL NEED
100g (4oz) plain flour
25g (1oz) margarine
25g (1oz) lard
Pinch of salt
Ice-cold water
Strawberry or apricot jam

1 Sieve the salt and flour into a large mixing bowl. Cut the margarine and lard into little cubes and drop them into the flour. Mix with a knife.

2 Rub the flour and fat together with your fingers until the mixture looks like breadcrumbs.

3 Sprinkle 2 tablespoons of water into the mixture. Stir in quickly with a palette knife. Add more water, if necessary. Now with your hands form the dough into a ball that leaves the bowl clean. Wrap the pastry in cling film and leave in the fridge for 30 minutes; this makes it easier to roll out. Turn the oven on to 190°C/375°F/Gas mark 5.

4 Sprinkle flour on to the work surface and the rolling pin. Gently roll out the pastry to 5mm (⅛in) thick. Cut the pastry into circles with the cutter and put into patty tins.

5 Put 1 teaspoon of jam into each tart and bake in the oven for about 15 minutes until the pastry is golden.

SAFETY TIP: *Make sure an adult helps you when using the oven.*

SAUSAGE AND APPLE PARCELS

Use your pastry-making skills to make these tasty, savoury pasties. Decorate them with pastry leaves and serve them cold as a party snack, or eat them hot with vegetables as a main meal. Make the pastry following the method used for Jam Tarts on page 72. Put the pastry in the fridge for 15 minutes before rolling out. Makes 12.

YOU WILL NEED
Shortcrust pastry
made with
225g (8oz) plain flour
and 100g (4oz) fat
225g (8oz) pork sausage meat
1 large cooking apple
100g (4oz) fresh breadcrumbs
1 small onion and 1 egg
Salt and pepper
Pinch of mixed herbs
Milk to glaze

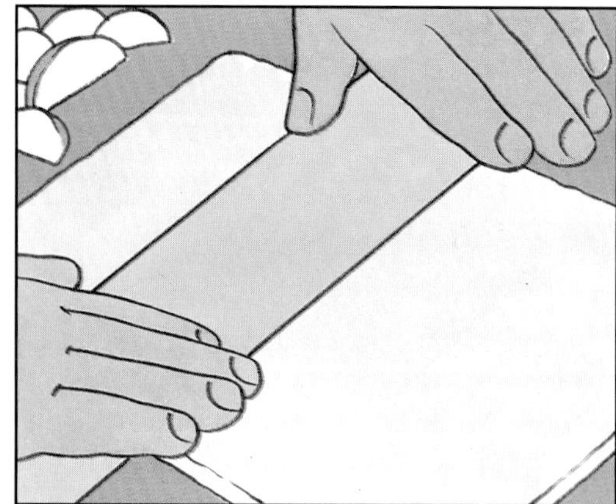

1 Make the pastry following the instructions on pages 72 and 73. Mix the sausage meat with the breadcrumbs. Peel and chop the onion and add to the sausage with the beaten egg and seasonings.

2 Peel, core and thickly slice the apple. Roll out the pastry on a floured surface and cut into 4 squares. Divide the sausage mix into 4 portions.

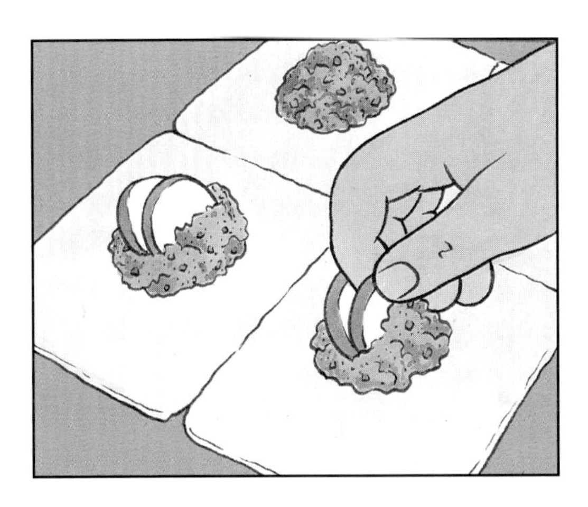

3 Turn the oven on to 220°C/ 425°F/Gas mark 7. Put one portion of the sausage stuffing and some apple slices on to the centre of one square of pastry.

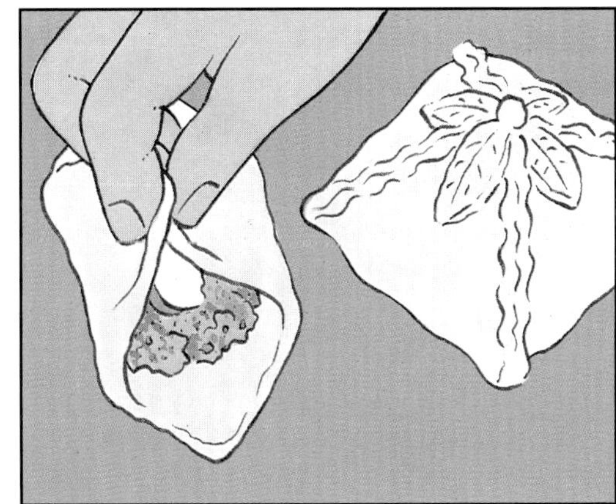

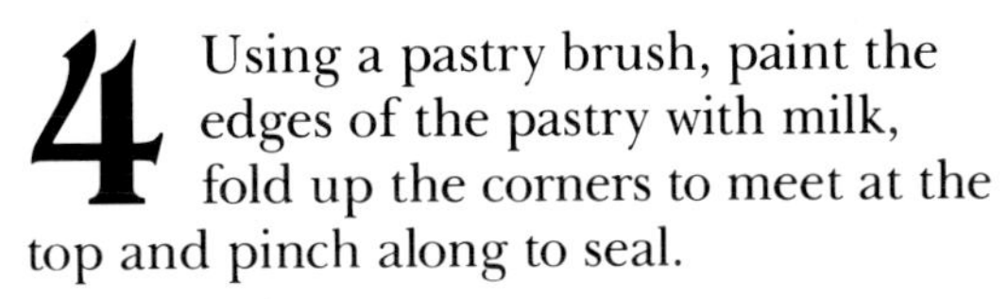

4 Using a pastry brush, paint the edges of the pastry with milk, fold up the corners to meet at the top and pinch along to seal.

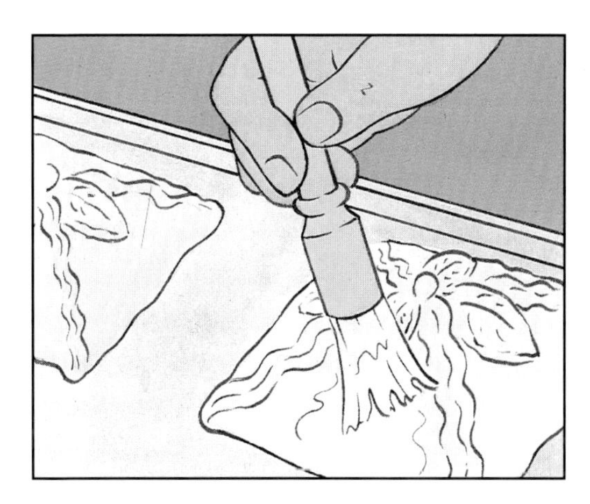

5 Make up the rest of the pasties in the same way, garnish with leaves made out of the left over pastry, and brush with milk to glaze. Put them on to a baking tray and bake in the oven for 15 minutes until golden brown.

SAFETY TIP: *Make sure an adult helps you when using a sharp knife and the oven.*

CEREAL CAKES

These cakes are really easy to make and need very little cooking. They're just cereals mixed with either melted chocolate or simple toffee made with butter and syrup. If you add chopped nuts or fruit it makes them even nicer. Makes 12.

1 For the chocolate covered cakes, break the chocolate into small pieces and put into a bowl. Place the bowl over a saucepan of boiling water and leave until the chocolate has completely softened.

2 Remove the bowl of chocolate from the saucepan. Add your chosen cereal and stir carefully until it is well covered with chocolate. Spoon into paper cake cases and leave for about an hour to set.

3 For the crunchy cakes, melt the butter and syrup in the saucepan and cook gently for about 5 minutes stirring occasionally.

YOU WILL NEED

Double Choc
75g (3oz) coco pops
100g (4oz) plain chocolate

Snow White Crispies
75g (3oz) rice crispies
100g (4oz) white chocolate drops

Nutty Flake Crunch
75g (3oz) butter
3 tablepoons golden syrup
50g (2oz) chopped mixed nuts
75g (3oz) bran flakes

Fruity Crunch
75g (3oz) corn flakes
50g (2oz) chopped glacé fruit
75g (3oz) butter
3 tablepoons golden syrup

SAFETY TIP: *Make sure an adult helps you when using the hob.*

4 Remove from the heat and stir in the cereals and nuts or fruit. Line a baking tin with non-stick baking paper and pour in the mixture. Press it down flat.

5 Leave to set for about half an hour then mark sections with a knife. When it is quite cool remove from the tin and break into segments and serve.

SWEET AND SAVOURY POPCORN

Recreate the magic of the cinema with a cone of popcorn to nibble as you watch a video. The recipe shows you how to pop the corn quickly and safely, and how to add butter and salt or whip up a crunchy candy topping.

1 Put about two handfuls of corn into a saucepan so that it just covers the bottom of the pan. Put the lid on and heat gently.

2 After a few minutes you will hear the corn beginning to pop. Don't take off the lid yet! Lift the pan from time to time and shake gently to speed up the popping.

3 When there has been no sound for about a minute, turn off the heat and remove the lid. Tip the corn into a dish and pick out any un-popped kernels.

SAFETY TIP: *Make sure an adult helps you when using the hob.*

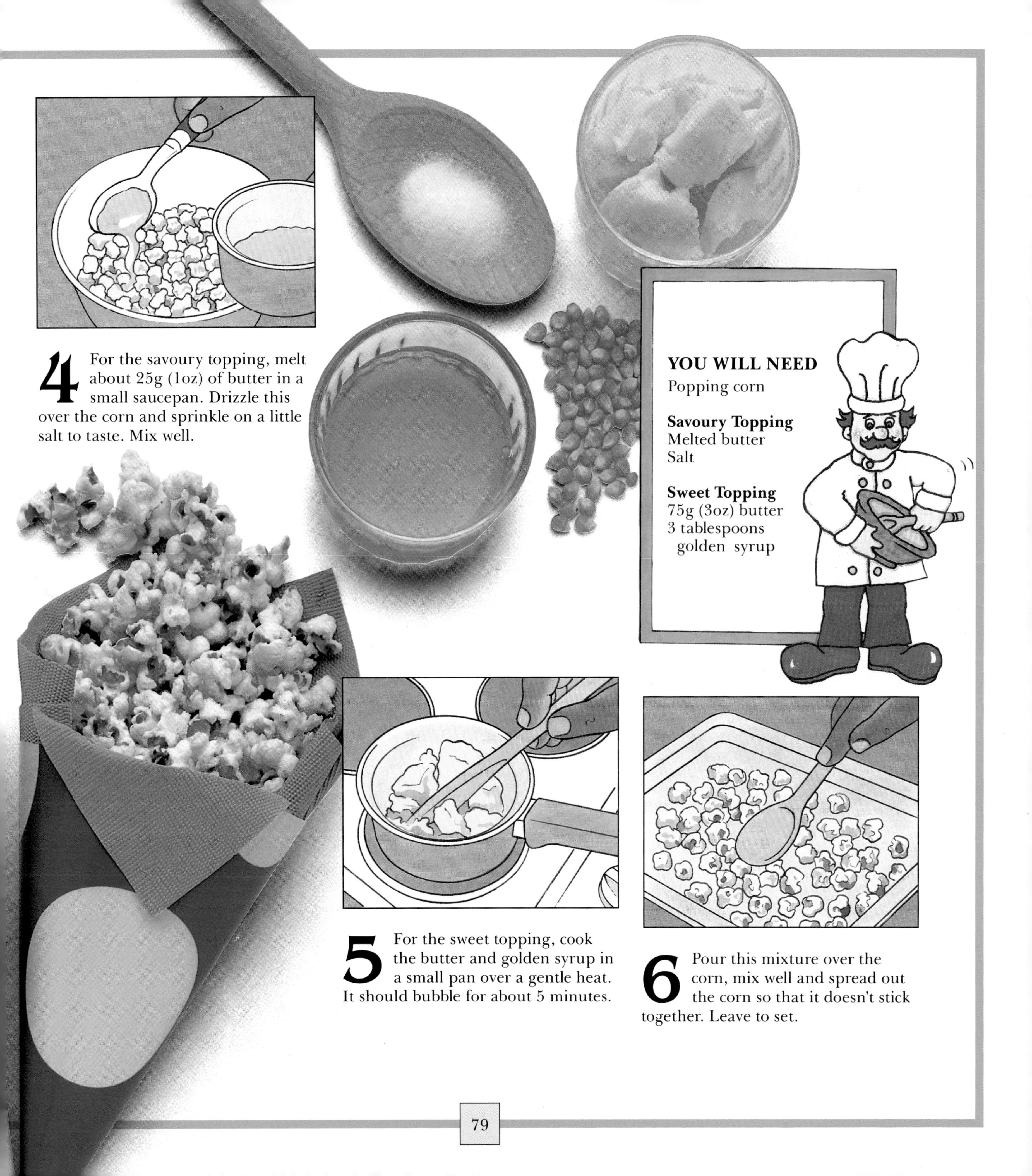

4 For the savoury topping, melt about 25g (1oz) of butter in a small saucepan. Drizzle this over the corn and sprinkle on a little salt to taste. Mix well.

YOU WILL NEED
Popping corn

Savoury Topping
Melted butter
Salt

Sweet Topping
75g (3oz) butter
3 tablespoons golden syrup

5 For the sweet topping, cook the butter and golden syrup in a small pan over a gentle heat. It should bubble for about 5 minutes.

6 Pour this mixture over the corn, mix well and spread out the corn so that it doesn't stick together. Leave to set.

PEPPERMINT CREAMS

A prettily wrapped box of peppermint creams makes a great birthday present. To add variety, dip some of the sweets in melted chocolate.

1 Using a whisk, beat the egg white until it is frothy. Now add a few drops of peppermint essence or oil, and a few drops of the green food colouring.

YOU WILL NEED

1 egg white
225-275g (8-10oz) icing sugar
Peppermint essence or oil (oil is stronger)
Green food colouring
100g (4oz) plain chocolate

SAFETY TIP: *Make sure an adult helps you when using the hob.*

2 Sift the icing sugar into a large bowl and blend in the egg mixture with a fork. Add more icing sugar if necessary to make a dough for rolling out. Knead until the dough is smooth.

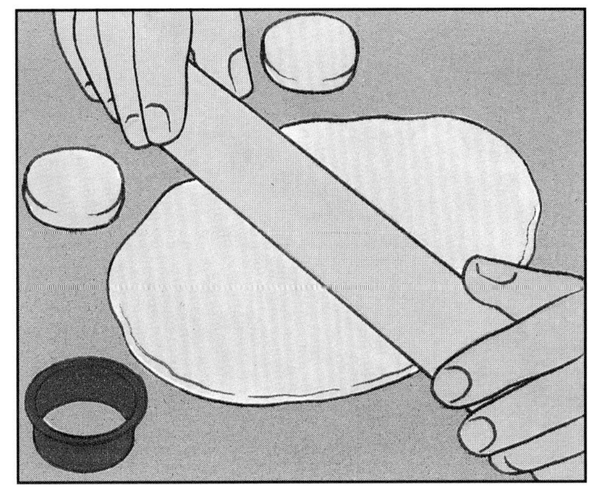

3 Dust your work surface and a rolling pin with icing sugar. Roll out the peppermint dough to about 1cm (3/8in) thick and cut out the peppermint creams with a round cutter. Cover a wire tray with greaseproof paper, put the sweets on it and leave to dry for about 1 hour.

4 Break up the chocolate into pieces and put into a small bowl. Boil some water in a saucepan, remove the pan from the heat and stand the bowl over it.

5 When the chocolate has melted stir it until it is smooth and then dip some of the sweets into it, coating just one half of the sweet in chocolate as shown. Leave to set, but not in the fridge.

MILK SHAKES

Milk shakes are wonderfully refreshing and nourishing too. Just one of these shakes with a sandwich, some cookies or fresh fruit will make the perfect quick snack whatever you're doing. If you are throwing a party, serve the shakes in tall attractive glasses with colourful straws and decorations. Each of the recipes here makes one milk shake.

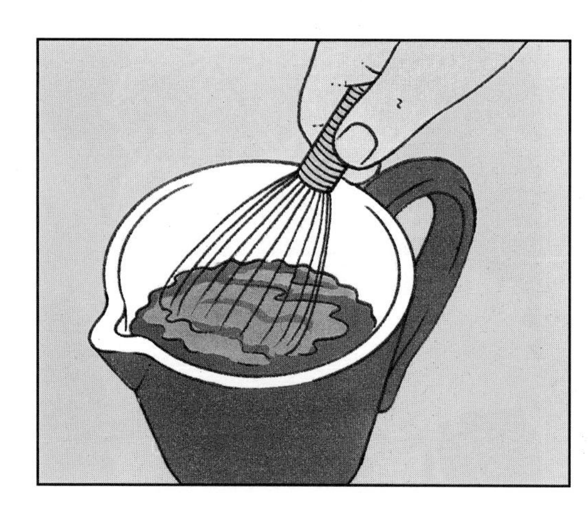

2 Whisk in the milk and ice-cream until it is frothy. Pour into a glass and sprinkle on the grated chocolate.

1 For the Rich Chocolate Shake, dissolve the cocoa powder and the sugar in a bowl or measuring jug with a little hot water. Stir well to blend.

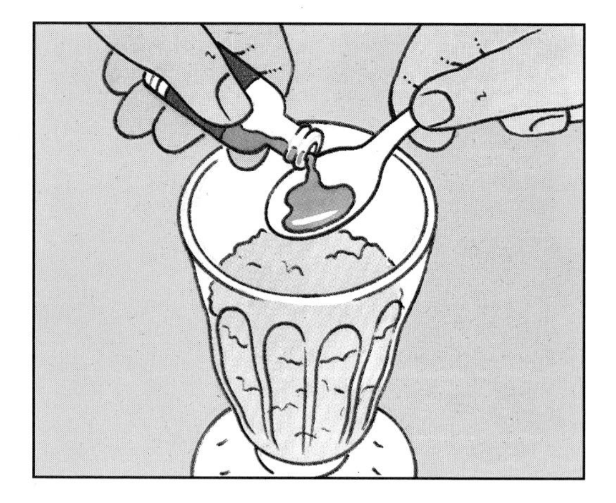

3 To make the Minty Milk, whisk all the ingredients together using about 3 drops of food colouring and ½ teaspoon of peppermint essence. Add a little caster sugar if you wish.

4 For the Continental Coffee, pour the hot water on to the coffee granules, add the sugar and mix in a bowl until completely dissolved. Put 4 ice cubes into a glass and add the coffee mixture. Pour the milk into the glass. Do not stir this milk shake. Sprinkle some grated chocolate on the top if you wish.

YOU WILL NEED

Rich Chocolate Shake
1 teaspoon cocoa powder
1 teaspoon caster sugar
275ml (½ pint) milk
A scoop of chocolate ice-cream
Grated chocolate

Milky Mint
275ml (½pint) milk
A scoop of mint choc-chip ice-cream
Green food colouring
Peppermint essence

Continental Coffee
150ml (5fl oz) milk
1 teaspoon instant coffee granules
2 teaspoons sugar
100ml (4fl oz) hot water

FEAST FOR FOUR

Once you have mastered some of the recipes in this book why not try making a complete three-course meal? On the following pages we have suggested a delicious menu for you to make for your friends or family. Most of the work can be done in advance to give you time to serve the food in style and enjoy eating it too!

MENU

Starter
Egg and Prawn Nests

•

Main course
Chicken and Vegetable Bake
Scallop Potatoes

•

Dessert
Fruit Pavlova

•

Coffee and Mints

EGG AND PRAWN NESTS

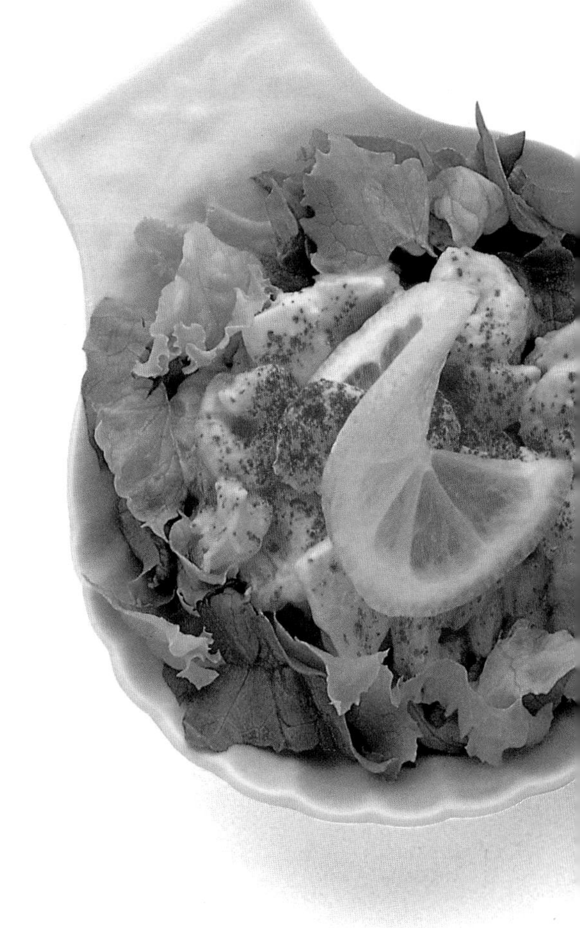

A favourite way to start a meal is with this tasty cocktail of chopped hard boiled egg mixed with prawns in a seafood sauce. Garnish with tiny triangles of brown bread and butter. Serves 4.

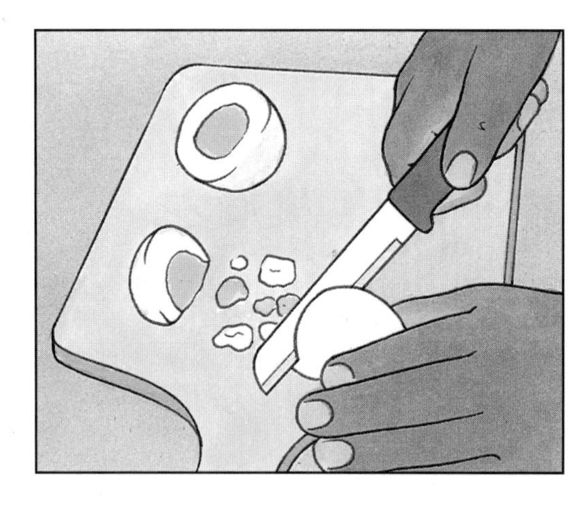

1 Put the eggs in a small saucepan and pour in enough cold water to cover them. Put on a high heat, bring to the boil and then reduce the heat to simmer for 10 minutes. Remove the pan from the heat and stand in cold water to cool. Peel off the shells and chop the eggs.

2 Wash and dry the lettuce and cut into shreds. Put into the base of the dishes to make a nest for the cocktail.

3 To make the seafood sauce, mix all the sauce ingredients together in a dish and stir well. Add the prawns and the chopped egg, and mix gently.

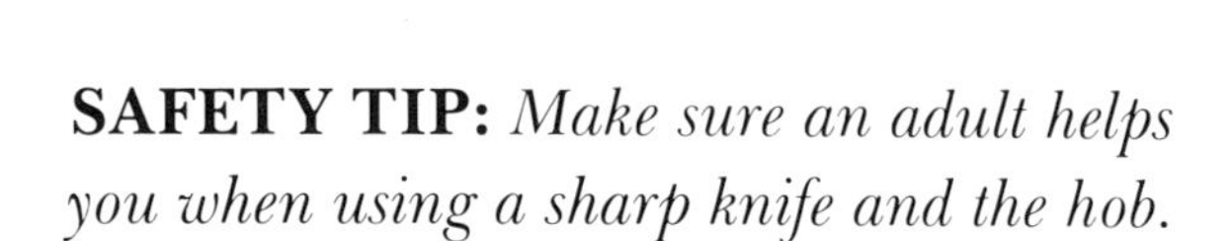

SAFETY TIP: *Make sure an adult helps you when using a sharp knife and the hob.*

YOU WILL NEED
2 eggs
175g (6oz) peeled fresh prawns

Seafood sauce
4 tablespoons mayonnaise
1 tablespoon tomato ketchup
1 tablespoon plain yoghurt
1 teaspoon lemon juice
A dash of Worcester sauce
Cayenne pepper
Salt and pepper
Some lettuce leaves

4 Divide the prawn mixture between the four dishes and decorate with slices of lemon and a sprinkle of cayenne pepper.

YOU WILL NEED
4 skinned chicken portions
2 tablespoons plain flour
2 tablespoons sunflower oil
4 bacon rashers
2 celery sticks
2 small parsnips
100g (4oz) small button mushrooms
4 large carrots
1 large onion
570ml (1pint) chicken stock made from a stock cube
1 tablespoon mushroom ketchup
1 teaspoon mixed herbs
Salt and pepper

CHICKEN AND VEGETABLE BAKE

This lovely warming casserole combines the vegetables and the meat in a tasty sauce. Serve it straight from the oven in an earthenware dish. Teamed with the Scallop potatoes (page 92) it makes a substantial and impressive main course. Serves 4.

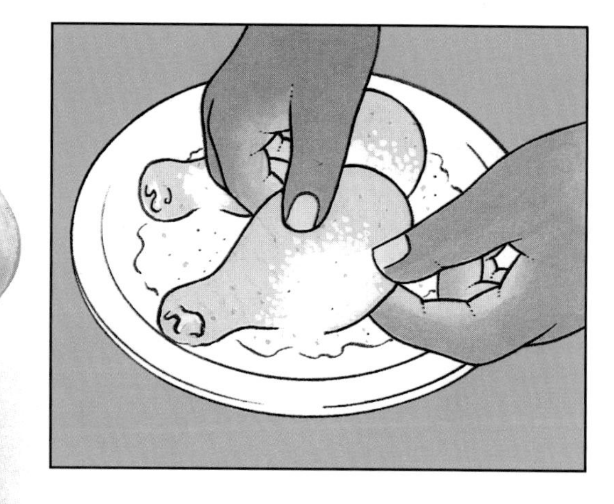

1 Mix the flour, salt, pepper and herbs on a plate. Roll the chicken portions in it to coat them completely.

SAFETY TIP: *Make sure an adult helps you when using a sharp knife, the hob and the oven.*

2 Chop the onion and bacon. Heat the oil in a frying pan. Add the onion and bacon and cook gently. Put in the chicken pieces and cook until brown. Transfer the chicken to a casserole dish. Turn the oven on to 170°C/325°F/Gas mark 3.

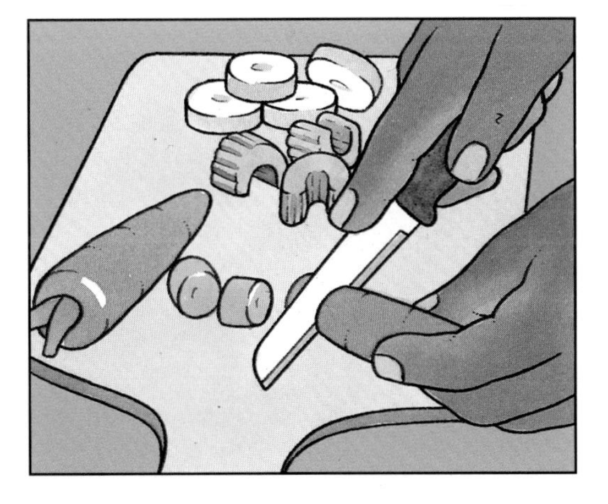

3 Peel and slice the carrots and parsnips and wash and chop the celery. Fry them gently in the pan then sprinkle on the remains of the seasoned flour and stir constantly for about 2 minutes.

4 Pour in the stock and stir thoroughly, scraping the pan to mix and thicken the sauce. Add the mushrooms and the mushroom ketchup.

5 Spoon all the ingredients very carefully into the casserole dish. Put on the lid and cook in the oven for about 1 hour 20 minutes.

SCALLOP POTATOES

This delicious potato dish is the perfect partner for the chicken and vegetable bake. Not only do they taste good together but you can cook them in the same oven, for the same length of time and serve them both from their cooking dishes. Serves 4.

1 Using the potato peeler, peel the potatoes and then slice them very thinly with a kitchen knife.

SAFETY TIP: *Make sure an adult helps you when using a sharp knife and the oven.*

2 Grease the base of the ovenproof dish and put in a layer of potatoes. Dot a little butter over them and sprinkle on some salt and pepper.

3 Continue to add layers of potato slices. Sprinkle each layer with salt and pepper and dot with butter.

YOU WILL NEED

900g (2lb) potatoes
25g (1oz) butter
290ml (½ pint) milk
1 teaspoon salt
Black pepper

4 Pour over the milk and add the last of the butter so that the top layer of potatoes will go crunchy when it is cooked. Cook in the oven with the chicken and vegetable bake for about 1 hour 20 minutes.

FRUIT PAVLOVA

What an impressive pudding, you'll hardly believe you made it yourself! A delicious meringue base, topped with a layer of whipped cream and whatever fresh fruit you fancy. Try strawberries, raspberries, kiwi fruit or a mixture of them all. Serves 4.

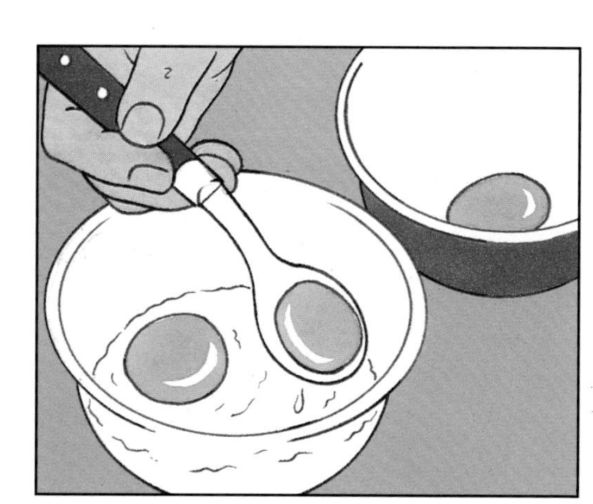

1 Break the eggs into a mixing bowl and carefully lift out the yolks with a spoon. It's very important that the bowl is free from grease and that there is absolutely no yolk mixed in with the whites.

YOU WILL NEED

3 large fresh egg whites
175g (6oz) caster sugar
275ml (½ pint) whipping cream
350g (12oz) soft fruit

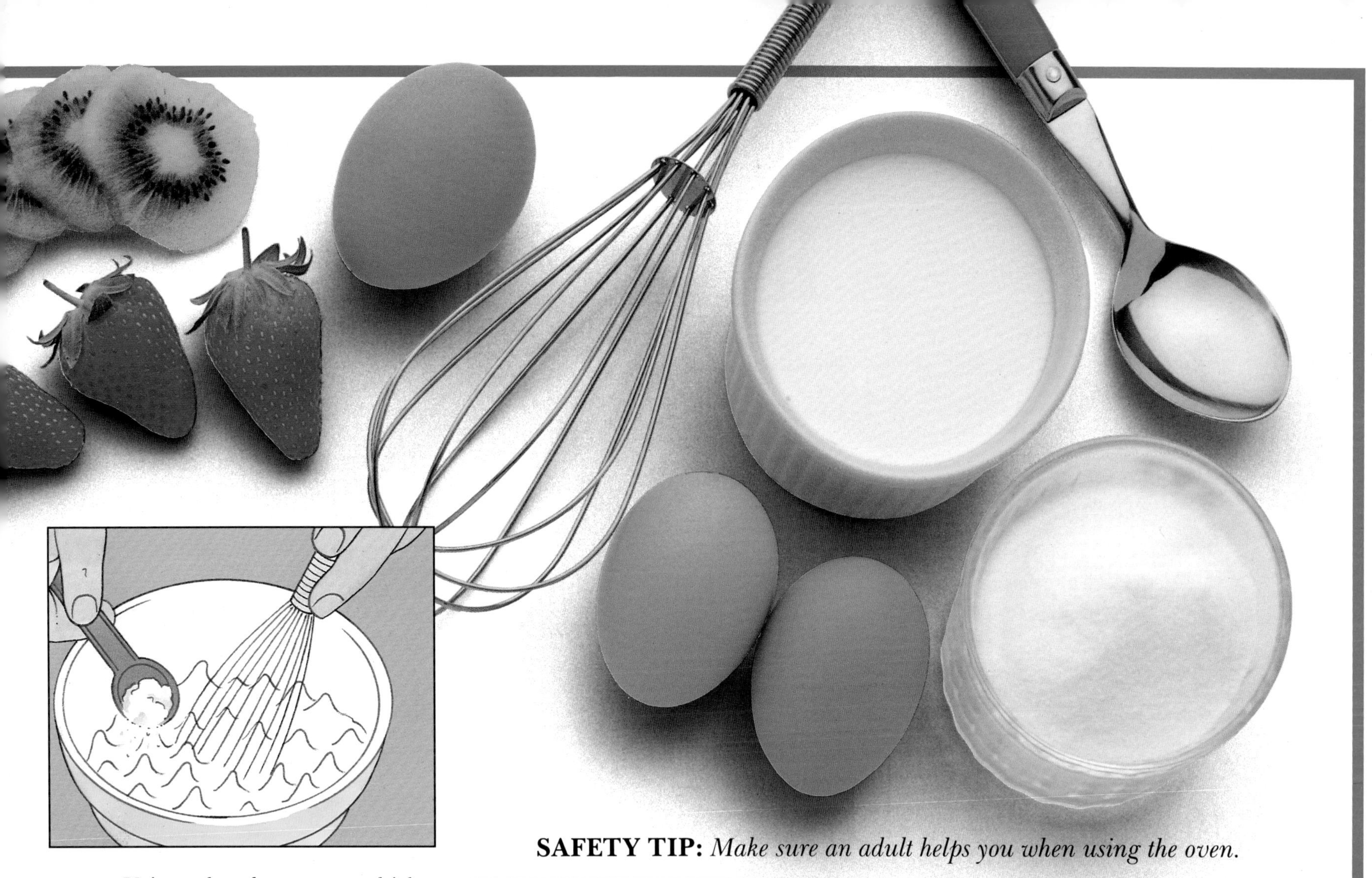

SAFETY TIP: *Make sure an adult helps you when using the oven.*

2 Using a hand or rotary whisk, beat the whites until they form soft peaks, then whisk in the sugar a tablespoon at a time. Turn on the oven to 150°C/300°F/Gas mark 2.

3 Lay a sheet of silicone paper on to a baking tray and carefully spoon the meringue on to it in a circle.

4 Make a dip in the centre of the meringue and draw up little peaks round the edge with the tip of a fork. Put into the oven and turn the temperature down to 140°C/275°F/Gas mark 1. Cook for 1 hour. Turn off the oven but leave the pavlova inside for at least 2 hours or overnight. Remove from oven and peel off the paper.

5 Using the whisk, whip the cream until it forms soft peaks. Just before serving, spoon the cream into the meringue case and decorate with the sliced fruit.

INDEX

B
Biscuits:
  Florentine **56-57**
  Shortbread **58-59**
Bread:
  Breakfast Rolls **20-21**
  Club Sandwiches **66-67**
  Garlic **38-39**
  Making **18-19**
  Open Sandwiches **68-69**
  Special Fried **10-11**
Breakfast Menus **10-21**
Breakfast Rolls **20-21**
Burgers **32-33**

C
Cakes:
  Cereal **76-77**
  Chocolate **64-65**
  Lemon Cheesecake **48-51**
  Sponge Cakes **60-61**
Carbohydrates **8**
Cereal Cakes **76-77**
Chicken:
  Tandoori **28-29**
  and vegetable bake **90-91**
Chocolate:
  Cake **64-65**
  Milk Shake **84-85**
Cleanliness in the kitchen **6**
Club Sandwiches **66-67**
Coffee Milk Shake **84-85**
Cooking Terms **7**
Crêpes, *see* Pancakes

D
Drinks **82-85**

E
Egg:
  and Prawn Nests **88-89**
  Rumble Tumble **12-13**
Exotic Fruit Salad **52-53**

F
Fairy Cakes **60-61**
Fats **8**
Fibre **9**
Fish Pie **34-35**
Florentine Biscuits **56-57**
Frankfurter Faces **22-23**
Fruit:
  Cocktails **82-83**
  Pavlova **94-95**
  Salad **52-53**
Fruity Cocktails **82-83**

G
Garlic Bread **38-39**
Glacé Icing **60-61**

J
Jam Tarts **72-73**

K
Kebabs **26-27**

L
Lemon Cheesecake **48-51**

M
Main Meals **22-45, 86-95**
Marzipan Magic **62-63**
Measuring ingredients **6**
Meringue, *see* Pavlova
Milk Shakes **84-85**
Minerals **9**
Muesli **14-15**

O
Open Sandwiches **68-69**

P
Pancakes:
  savoury **30-31**
  sweet **16-17**
Party time menus **66-85**
Pasta **40-41**
Pastry **72-73**
Pavlova **94-95**
Peppermint:
  Creams **80-81**
  Milkshake **84-85**
Pizza, Patterned **42-43**
Popcorn, sweet and savoury **78-79**
Potatoes:
  baked **24-25**
  scallop **92-93**
Prawns, *see* Egg and Prawn Nests
Proteins **8**

R
Ratatouille **38-39**
Rice, spicy **36-37**
Rumble Tumble Egg **12-13**

S
Safety **6**
Salad, sweet and savoury **44-45**
Sauces:
  Seafood **88-89**
  Tomato and Herb **40-41**
Sausage and Apple Parcels **74-75**
Scones **54-55**
Seafood Sauce **88-89**
Shortbread **58—59**
Special Fried Bread **10-11**
Spinach-filled Pancakes **30-31**

T
Tandoori Chicken **28-29**
Teatime menus **46-65**
Three-course meal **86-95**
Toasted Sandwiches **70-71**
Tomato and Herb Sauce **40-41**
Trifle, English **46-47**

V
Vitamins **9**